Morten Bay

HOMO CONEXUS

- The Connected Humans

Homo Conexus

-The Connected Humans

By Morten Bay

Editorial assistance: Michelle Willrich, Dean Christopher and Martin Høybye

ISBN: 978-1-4710-9552-8

Originally Published in Danish by Gyldendal Business, Copenhagen 2009

Cover Design: Rasmus Blæsbjerg, HAUS, Los Angeles

CONTENTS

The little boy looked up at his dad and said: "Dad, if you didn't have computers back when you were a kid, how did you get online?"

FOREWORD

"Now, everybody here, we're all familiar with Facebook. It's a website that the kids use to coordinate which malt shop to meet up at after their sock hop...I'M OLD! And of course, those kids' parents use it to stay up all night looking at what their high school girlfriends are up to, composing heartfelt friends request messages, only to delete them unsent."

This was how Jon Stewart opened the first segment on Comedy Central's The Daily Show on January 6th 2011. Stewart wisely avoids pretending that he's at the forefront of what the kids are doing on their cell phones or laptops, just like most of us do in order to avoid ridicule. However, funny as they are, Stewart's two opening lines from that January episode contain several misconceptions, even with the popular comedian's usual caveats about being an old guy who doesn't understand the kids.
First of all, Facebook is not just a website. It's a website, an iPhone app, a mobile platform, a meeting place, a dating service, a business opportunity and a gaming arena. It is no longer contained within the computer screen. And it's definitely not just the kids who use it. Or their parents, whom Stewart hangs out to dry with awesome wit. It's kids, parents, and grandparents, everybody uses Facebook now. In 2010, a study by InsideFacebook.com showed that not only did 100 million Americans – almost one third of the population - use Facebook. 18.4 million of those were older than 45, meaning that every fifth person on Facebook is a grandparent or a parent. Needless to say, the 18-35-year olds are the heaviest users, with almost as many users being over 26 years old than under. The vast majority of Facebook users are 26 and over. So if you think Facebook is just something the kids use, you're dead wrong. In fact, the misunderstanding that all the gadgets, online phenomena, cultural changes or technological advances of the past 10 years are something "that the kids use" is generally wrong. And yet every time something new shows up, everyone

seems to think it's a "Generation Y trend" or something the "technologically hip kids" are getting into. But if you look at Twitter, the iPad or localization services like Foursquare and Facebook Places, it's usually adults who take it up first. Kids still mostly just text and call on their cell phones, maybe taking a photo once in a while. So are you just out of touch because you never get into the latest tech trend a year after everyone else?

No. There is absolutely nothing wrong with you.

What you are witnessing is the emergence of a new type of human being. One that – across different age groups and social conditions – handles the rapid changes of our society more naturally than other people. It's a type of human for whom networking is as natural as breathing, and whose self-understanding and existence is dependent on others in his or her network. They are not technological wunderkinds, but rather use or discard technology at will. They shop different, work different, communicate different, and think different from people who are still rooted in the Industrial Society. As such, they represent a new consumer audience, a new type of co-worker and a new recipient of communication, marketing and advertising messages. Reaching out to them is a new challenge to anyone trying to sell a product or change political persuasions. New rules apply. A lot has been written and said about how to communicate with Generation N, Z, The Network Generation, The Millenials, Digital Natives, whatever you want to call them. How to get them to buy your product. How to change their minds about something. Apparently, something has changed that renders the old methods useless. But little thought has been given to why this change is happening. And why it is happening now? And what kind of impact is it going to have on our lives in the long run? Yes, we all agree that we are now in the Information Age or the Network Society rather than the industrial society. But how did this change come about? And is it all good? How will it change us as human beings? The last question is the most important one for this book. On the following pages, a history of the Network Society is told and a lot of thinking about what this societal change does to us on a personal level will be brought forth. In this book, this new citizen of the Network Society is regarded as a different type of Homo Sapiens. And that's why they're called Homo Conexus. Many people don't understand why it is necessary to be texting at the dinner table, and they consider young people's habits of multitasking to be rude. And why do they post unimportant trivialities about themselves on Twitter all the time? And what's this thing about uploading all those private photos on Facebook for everyone to see? And telling everyone where they located all the time by checking in on Foursquare and Facebook Places? Have they no sense of privacy? Indeed, in recent years, if you are to believe the mainstream media, a digital divide has appeared between young people and their parents. And a lot of people are having trouble understanding what is going on. This book is for them. This book is not for the people it is about. They are in the know already. This book is for those parents who want to understand why their teenagers are acting as they do. It is for the employer who is having trouble motivating or communicating with his twenty-something employees. It is for those marketing execs who want a better understanding of why their message is not striking a chord with people below the age of 40. And it is for those in their early or mid-thirties who never understood why they looked at the world differently, in a more forward-thinking way than their peers. Hopefully, when you reach the final pages of this book, I will have managed to convince you that our society and human beings in general are changing dramatically for better or worse, forcing us to rethink almost everything. But if you at this point are still not convinced that rapid changes are going on, let me just for a short while return to Jon Stewart and the January 6th episode of The Daily Show. The reason why Stewart was talking about Facebook at all, was because investment bank Goldman Sachs had started investing in Facebook on behalf of its clients. And as of the morning of January 6th, Facebook didn't want to divulge anything about those investments. Jon Stewart, appropriately, called the company out on forcing its users to lead

transparent lives on their profiles, without wanting to be transparent itself. But Stewart and his crew hadn't even finished taping the show, when Facebook announced that they were going to be transparent about all their finances going forward. Jon Stewart had to end his show with a disclaimer which totally ruptured the balloon he had inflated earlier in the show. That's how fast things move today. And as we shall see over the coming pages, this acceleration of how we communicate and connect with each other is exactly what has created a whole new world. Just like it did when Gutenberg turbo-charged the educational level of the common man by revolutionizing the printing press almost 600 years ago.
It's happening now. Again.

Morten Bay,

Los Angeles, January 2011.

INTRODUCTION: WELCOME TO THE NETWORK SOCIETY

The *Christmas No. 1* is a big thing in the United Kingdom.

Having the number one song on the UK singles charts in the week leading up to Christmas shows that you've conquered the holiday sales – which traditionally is when the most music is sold during the year. It's been something music artists in the UK have strived for since 1952 when the chart was founded.

The Beatles won the prestigious chart position three years in a row in 1963-1965. Queen's *Bohemian Rhapsody* was the *Christmas no. 1* in 1975. Pink Floyd's *Another Brick in the Wall pt. 2* made it in 1979. In 1982 it was *Don't You Want Me* by The Human League. In 1995 it was *Earth Song* by Michael Jackson. In 2003, Gary Jules' beautiful reworking of *Mad World* by Tears for Fears got the prestigious honor. All of them major worldwide hits, which shows why the UK *Christmas No. 1* is such an indicator of popularity.

But then, something happened.

In 2005, Shayne Ward's *That's My Goal* went to number one over Christmas. You might not know this name, which is totally understandable, because Ward wasn't very popular outside Great Britain. You see, he was the winner of that year's *The X Factor* competition. The TV reality show is widely regarded as the European version of *American Idol*, and like its American counterpart, it is partly owned and operated by music entrepreneur Simon Cowell. Only once before, in 2002, had the winners of a TV reality show/talent competition taken the number one spot over Christmas. Otherwise, that sacred ground on the charts had been reserved for *real* artists or for charity singles. But things had changed. The reality talent show tidal wave had flooded the world, and this was also the case in the English Isles.

In fact, the power of reality talent shows – and especially those owned by Cowell – was so immense that charts all over the world were impacted by them. In the UK, this meant that the *Christmas no. 1* singles in 2005, 2006, 2007 and 2008 were all released by *X Factor* winners.

But then something happened. Again.

In 2009, the *Christmas no. 1* single was a 17-year old song by a group that had never been even been in the UK top 20 before. It was the highly aggressive and not very Christmas-y *Killing In The Name* by the American rap/metal group Rage Against the Machine. Poor Joe McElderry, 18 years old at the time, had won *The X Factor* in 2009, and still wasn't going to make it to the top. Instead, the aggressive chants of *"F*** You, I won't do what you tell me!!"* that is the culmination of *Killing In The Name* was the best-selling single over Christmas, selling 52.000 more than McElderry's single *The Climb*.

How did *that* happen?

Rage Against the Machine hadn't even reissued the song as a single, but to their surprise, they were number one in the UK over Christmas 2009. The reasons for this surprising turn of events say everything about the time that we are living in right now. And why it might be time for us all to stop and think about what's going on. Jon and Tracy Morter are two British music fans who have followed the charts all their lives. But the predictability of the *X Factor* winners grabbing the number one spot over Christmas year after year was killing the excitement of the Christmas chart race for them. So they decided to do something about it. When Joe McElderry looked like he was heading for the number one spot with *The Climb* (A Miley Cyrus cover, which apparently made things worse for the Morters), the couple went on Facebook and started a group for people who wanted to change the status quo.

The Facebook group was introduced with the words:

"Fed up of Simon Cowell's latest karaoke act being Christmas No 1? Me too ... So who's up for a mass-purchase of the track 'Killing In The Name' as a protest to the X Factor monotony?"

Apparently, a lot of people were fed up. Within days, the group snowballed into having hundreds of thousands of members. And in the week leading up to December 19, the deadline for sales to be registered for the Christmas week chart, *Killing In The Name* sold 500,000 copies. 200,000 of those in just two days. This was a grassroots movement on steroids. People who were tired of the pop establishment had risen up to have their say. But they had done so faster than ever before.

And it was only possible because we now live in the Network society.

Had someone attempted to pull off a *coup d'etat* on the British music charts just ten years earlier, there was no way they could have succeeded. First of all, it would have required that everyone involved had to go out to a store and buy a physical cd-version of *Killing In the Name*. And since that song is 17 years old, the chances of finding a single like that in stores (even ten years ago) would have been zero. On top of that, you would have to pull the Brits out of their warm homes and into the cold winter weather. That's a hard task if any. Finally, you would have had to spend millions of dollars on an information or ad campaign that would have taken months to get people hooked. Either that or you would have had to convince national TV stations like the BBC to carry your message, which is just about as difficult as finding the money for the ad campaign. And still, the Morters managed to move 502.000 copies of *Killing In The Name* in just a couple of weeks. Because nowadays, music sales are digital, instant and available from the comfort of your own home. You can even buy music directly on your smartphone, download and listen to it within seconds. So no venturing outside into the cold, British winter was necessary. Next, the 500 million-plus users on Facebook and the strength of viral communication made it possible for the Morters to get to a lot of people –*fast* – without spending anything more than time and a broadband fee. But really, the reason why the UK charts were hit by this tremendously surprising attack is because we've changed as human beings. You see, The Morters are in their mid-thirties, which puts them among the oldest members of the demographic known as Generation N, or *Digital Natives*. Or as I call them in this book, *Homo Conexus*. They are connected in ways their parents weren't. They think differently from people just a few years older than them. They look at the world and especially themselves differently. They feel empowered in ways no individuals have before. And they are prime members of the Network Society. This is a demographic that a lot of people in recent years have had a hard time understanding. That's why corporations have spent a lot of money on consultants like the author of this book in order to understand the habits and new consumer manners of this young and young adult demographic. You would think that *The X Factor* winners would now be banned forever from the top of the UK music charts at Christmas, right? Not so. Because when Christmas 2010 came around, something very typical for the Network Society happened, which actually took that year's *The X Factor* winner, Matt Cardle, to #1. The Network Society is all about decentralization as a megatrend. This is something this book will dive into in much further detail later on, but for now, here's how decentralization paved the way for Matt Cardle and his *When We Collide* single: Based on the success of the Morters' campaign, a flurry of initiatives was available this time around. One Facebook initiative would have people buy *4'33"*, a piece by John Cage containing nothing but silence. Another initiative wanted to put *Surfin' Bird* by The Trashmen on top, in an odd homage to the animated TV series *Family Guy*. A third initiative tried to get metal group Pantera to #1. And so on. Because the music fans who voted with their wallets in the race for the UK Christmas number one were spread out over several different pieces of music, no one song could beat the popularity of Matt Cardle. The Rage Against The Machine campaign came into existence in an attempt to decentralize Simon Cowell's power over the British charts. But then, *that idea* became a central power that needed to be decentralized. And thus, the music buyers spread themselves over too many Christmas singles to make an impact. Back in the early part of the last decade, everyone was talking about convergence. That we would see technologies converging towards each other and finally merging so one device could do everything. But even though we now have phones that can do almost everything but make the coffee, we still find ourselves surrounded by game consoles where you can use your body as a controller, flat screen TV's with apps like the ones for smart phones and tablets that compliment our laptops. Technology didn't converge. It got decentralized. Because of this decentralization, many people find it stressful and exhausting to keep up with the flurry of new media out there, from handheld devices to social media on the web to the high-tech gadgetry now required just to watch your favorite show on TV. And yet, certain types of people across all age brackets seem to be taking it in their stride. Even relishing in the many opportunities the Network Society offers. Like most people, I used to believe that modern consumer technology, hipness and youth were concepts that belonged together. But then, a couple of years ago, a string of events had me examine the matter, only to find that I was dead wrong.

To explain, I'm afraid I have to return to Simon Cowell.

Social Media Un-hipsters

On April 11th, 2009, television audiences all across the United Kingdom sat down to watch the season opener of *Britain's Got Talent*, another amateur talent showcase created by Simon Cowell, which spawned off *America's Got Talent*. This was the

UK show's third season, following a second season that had turned out to be bland and disappointing.

You see, there hadn't been a Paul Potts in 2008.

Paul Potts was an unassuming cell phone salesman from Wales who stunned everyone when he first walked on stage, unleashing a tenor voice that rivaled the vocal instruments of the world's foremost opera singers. Potts went on to win 1st Prize in 2007. Unique, surprising and heartwarming. But what happened immediately after Potts's first performance is what makes the story *really* significant. His audition was so engaging, so moving and compelling, that, less than 24 hours later, his performance began burning up YouTube. And so, even before he won the competition – even before anyone outside the UK had even seen that particular episode of *Britain's Got Talent* – Paul Potts was famous all over Europe! Nowadays, a viral internet phenomenon like Paul Potts is not a rare occurrence. It's part of our daily amusement from amateur videos of a poor kid reacting to medication after a visit to the dentist, to hilarious Old Spice commercials: *I'm on a horse!* And sometimes it moves us, like the story of Ted Williams, the homeless man with the golden voice. He got lifted out of poverty and living on the street and thrown into the media machinery and ended up with a job and a free entry into rehab courtesy of Dr. Phil. All because someone filmed him and put him on YouTube. Even before Potts, videos of impressive, amusing or just plain weird performances were spreading virally to the worldwide audience. Consider Gary "Numa Numa Kid" Brolsma, whose lip-synching, chair-dancing video of himself acting out The CDM Projects' *Dragostea Din Tei* shot him into internet celebrity status almost overnight. Or the Star Wars Kid. Or any number of dancing, laughing or "adorable" gurgling babies. Or simply a kitten on a piano. What was unique about the Paul Potts phenomenon was his target demographic. Against all expectations, Potts sang *opera*. And although some groups of teens and young adults online actually do enjoy opera, or at least might enjoy the novelty of a cell phone salesman with a godlike voice, it was *not* the young audience segment that spread the word about him. It was grown-ups. Seniors, even. This flew right in the face of what everyone – including the so-called "experts" – believed about the internet and social media at the time. People thought that social media platforms were only for tech-savvy, connected "digital natives". In other words, young people. As it turns out, this wasn't the case. How do we know? Well, first of all, when Paul Potts released his debut album, *One Chance*, after his 2007 victory on *Britain's Got Talent*, it quickly became an international smash hit. It went to #1 on the charts in Australia, Korea, Germany, Ireland, New Zealand, Sweden and Norway. It rose to #3 in Mexico, #5 in Spain and #2 in the Netherlands. Even on the most coveted chart in the world, the USA's hard-to-crack *Billboard Top 200*, the album reached a very impressive #23! And all of this even without *Britain's Got Talent* airing anywhere outside the UK. It didn't stop there. TV stations all around the world picked up on the Potts phenomenon. The singer/salesman found himself on the *Oprah* and a host of other U.S. and international TV shows. This, of course, helped spur more album sales. But he would never have gotten the chance to be on these shows, and sell all those albums, except for all those mature, opera-loving internet users around the world, spreading the video of this improbable operatic sensation. But, just as many of us were assuming that the Paul Potts phenomenon was a one-time, sensational event that could happen only once, guess what?

It happened again!

When all those UK televiewers *tuned in* on April 11th, 2009 for the Season Three opener of *Britain's Got Talent*, they were hoping for another Paul Potts. They were hungry for another performer to not only defy conventional looks and behavior, but also give senior YouTube users a chance; once again, to make their presence felt in the social media realm.

And boy, did they get that chance!

18

Susan Boyle, a 47-year old Scottish woman, took the stage to sing *I Dreamed a Dream*, from the hit musical *Les Misérables*. She seemed unlike anyone who should be on stage, based on popular notions of what a "singing star" should look like. She embodied visual characteristics stereotypically associated with folks descended from a long line of Scotsmen: a sturdy build; an unruly mane of hair; smallish, dark eyes; uncompromising eyebrows; teeth that were far from perfect and a ruddy complexion. But all that was forgotten the instant she opened her mouth to sing. An angel's voice soared above the audience, spellbinding them, literally bringing tears to their eyes. *Britain's Got Talent* had another Paul Potts on their hands. But this time, seniors on the web were more ready to deal with the phenomenon. Just four days after her appearance on the show, fifteen million people had watched her *Britain's Got Talent* audition on *YouTube*. Within nine days, that number would rise to over 100 million views. As with Paul Potts, there was absolutely nothing in Susan Boyle's looks or voice that would seem likely to appeal to a young audience. Neither were her song choices exactly targeted on a teen or young adult audience. In demographic terms, her target audience was definitely at very youngest the 30+ cohorts. In other words, grown-ups. Now, here's what's interesting about those "grown-ups" on YouTube. There are as many of them as there are teens. According to the Quantcast website tracking service, as of May 2010. 16% of all US YouTube users were more than 50 years old. 22% were between 35 and 49. And almost the same percentage, 21%, applies to the 13-17 year olds.

Okay, to be reasonable: there are *many* more people older than 50 than people between 13 and 17. But the fact that YouTube audiences 35 and younger make up 57%, and those older than 35 make up 38%, only goes to show that the young audiences are no longer a huge majority in the social media space. They're still the majority, yes, but in no way overly dominating. It certainly flies in the face of the notion that social media is only a trend amongst the young. And sure enough in August 2010, Pew Research Center's Internet and American Life Project revealed a survey that showed that 42% of seniors were now engaged in some sort of online social networking – primarily Facebook. The stories of Potts and Boyle show how the network society is now such a big part of everyone's everyday life. The reach of one's words and actions, and the ability to seek knowledge, are now virtually unlimited. And we're all part of this revolutionary new reality, for better or worse. Like it or not. That said, there are obviously some among us who have a better understanding of the Network Society than others. Especially young people who have grown up during this time can't believe that life was ever any different, any less interconnected. Their sense of reality stems from the fact that the whole world literally is at their fingertips. From this accelerated reality springs a special consciousness that everything is possible. Reality is flexible to them. It's bound together in a network that they can travel from point to point. If one stop doesn't satisfy them, they can simply move on to the next. Their consciousness is broader, their priorities are different, their ability to concentrate is keener, and their grip on the world is lighter. They *embody* the network structure in ways the rest of us will never understand. And this takes them beyond mere conscious thinking, which defined Homo Sapiens.

Their lives are defined by their connectedness.

They are the Connected Humans – *Homo Conexus*.

They are different from those who still stick to the values of the Industrial society. The sole purpose of this book is to help people understand Homo Conexus and the Network Society.

But in order to do that, I will have to take you back in time. The Network Society did not start with the breakthrough of the Internet. As we shall see in the following chapters, our conscious utilization of what is really a world of networks (that have always been here), started right after World War II. It started with the discovery that the brain is really a network, then it grew through the invention of cell phones, computer networks, satellite TV until we finally got to a place where it no longer makes sense to distinguish between any of our connected devices. And in recent years, the discoveries of networks in our bodies and nature have made enormous contributions to physics, medical and social science and our understanding of how the world works and human beings function. All of this will be revealed on the following pages, as I take you on a journey of the history of the Network Society and how Homo Conexus came to be. After that, I will show explain the differences between Industrial Man and Homo Conexus by placing Homo Conexus in settings you already know. But first, it is important to understand how major events and changes in our lives impact us as we grow up. By understanding *cohort theory* you may come to understand how certain values stick with us and some don't. And why there may be less cause for concern than you think. You see, at the core of all the tumbles and turmoil of the transition from The Industrial Society to The Network Society is the concept of *sudden acceleration*. The Network Society came into effect because our communications capabilities got accelerated very abruptly, seen over centuries of time.

But that has actually happened once before.

CHAPTER ONE:

A NEW RENAISSANCE

In 1503 there was a big and boisterous wedding amongst the "jet set" of the time in Florence, Italy. The rich weaver Angelo Doni was to marry his beloved Maddalena Strozzi, daughter of one of Tuscany's most powerful families. Doni loved art. He was one of the benefactors who supported Tuscany's Renaissance painters financially, regularly commissioning art works. (In 1505 he would have his portrait painted by the great Raphael.) Doni's wedding was to be special. To celebrate his nuptials, he approached one of the most sought-after artists, Michelangelo Buonarroti, to make a painting of the holy family – Mary, Joseph and the baby Jesus. At this time, Michelangelo was finishing one of his most revered sculptures – the statue of David, which was destined to stand in front of Palazzo Vecchio, Florence's city hall. Michelangelo's whole life to this point had been dedicated to marble and sculptures. But Doni wanted him to create an oil painting. This proved to be no problem for Michelangelo, who managed to get a double fee for his work, although Doni had tried to get him to do the job for half price. Sometimes artists do know how to bargain! In earlier years, Michelangelo had studied painting, but had stuck mostly to sketching. But the painting he did for his patron, now known as the *Doni Tondo,* is a heart-wrenchingly beautiful and – for its time – technically superior painting. It is the first real Michelangelo painting we know of. Although it is said to have had little respect for painting as an art, Michelangelo went on to become as famous for his paintings as for his sculptures. At the time, it seemed overwhelming that someone who was a talented and experienced sculptor should be so easily persuaded to take on a painting project. Indeed, such an enterprise would require a virtually divine talent – which, in fact, many thought Michelangelo did have, upon seeing his work at the Sistine Chapel. But his painting skill alone wasn't the issue. Our point is rather that Michelangelo was a true Renaissance Being. Early 16th Century Italy was a fantastic hotbed for the development of man. The individual communities and city-states were far from democratic. But after the Black Plague had finished savaging Italy, there was a greater openness among the rich and powerful towards everything that enriched life – including art and literature. At the same time, antique scriptures surfaced when medieval monasteries were cleaned out after the ravages of the plague. Ideas from earlier thinkers were given new life, thanks to poets and writers like Dante and Machiavelli. Knowledge was no longer monopolized by the church, and the financing of fresh thinking came from wealthy families – the patrons of change. This is why Michelangelo was able to educate himself sufficiently to paint the *Doni Tondo*. This was a new development in the history of Man. The recognition that *one man could excel in more than a single area,* was quite revolutionary, but even more so was the notion that *any man could educate himself*. This empowerment of the individual was quite a radical concept in that day and age. The same development took place, perhaps even more so, in the case of Michelangelo's elder rival Leonardo da Vinci, whose genius embraced engineering, philosophy and physics as well as the art of painting. Da Vinci and Michelangelo are the main examples of what we call "Renaissance Men." Meaning men who utilized the new tools at their disposal to break free from religious dogma and the conformities of their era.

Industrial Man

There's a straight line from the emancipations of the Renaissance to modern man. From the Renaissance grew the Enlightenment, with its uncoupling of religion from the autocracy of the aristocracy. Perhaps the most revolutionary technology to come out of the Renaissance was Johann Gutenberg's contribution to the world: The invention of movable type. The monopoly on the distribution of knowledge was broken, so that it was no longer just kings and churches who defined the truth. As a consequence, education was democratized, although it would take many years for it to become truly widespread. This was the founding principle which also paved the way for Renaissance Man: the possibility of – and the freedom to be – seeking new knowledge, and acquiring skills from books that were no longer the sole product of a hard working monk's decade of handwriting. Books containing knowledge could be made more quickly, in more copies, and be distributed wider and faster. This revolutionary new technology sparked discussions across borders, which in turn prompted the philosophical dialogue of the Enlightenment across Germany, England and France. Also originating in the Renaissance are the philosophical foundations upon which we have built our self-understanding. For instance, the works of philosopher René Descartes depict man as a subject who is not only conscious of his surroundings, but who inherently seeks to make sense of them. Gutenberg's gift to the world raised awareness levels and heightened the intellectual discourse in Europe, creating the foundation for modern society all the way into the twentieth century. Renaissance Man as a concept came and went. Still, the developments of the Renaissance were the catapult that propelled humanity into a new era, literally a rebirth – a re-nascence – of Man.

And this is the development we're witnessing once again.

Just like Gutenberg's invention of movable type centuries ago, an abrupt acceleration of how we share knowledge is propelling us forward as human beings, creating new ways of understanding the world, new cultures, new habits, new values. Just like in the 16th Century Renaissance, mankind is now experiencing another emancipation from the ties that bind the spread of knowledge. The internet and the cellular phone have democratized mass media, so that all who have something to say can say it to the whole world. And the dizzying speed by which the spread of information happens now makes it hard for political regimes to keep their people believing blindly and unquestioningly in whatever truth the regime offers. This astonishing velocity also means that new ideas – good and bad – are developed very quickly, and for that same reason there are more of them. People can come together across previously unheard-of distances, in networks that can produce new knowledge, new ideas and new initiatives, like a unified collective. Whether it be good, altruistic projects like Kiva.org where individuals can issue microloans to businesses in the third world, or less morally palatable objectives like the creation of international terrorist networks, the rise of new networks has taken reality to a whole new level. A modern-day analog of Gutenberg and his movable type. If entering the network society is entering a new Renaissance, then we will likely see an equally important and mind-broadening development in the near future, as the one experienced between the 13th and the 17th centuries. But this time it isn't just a question of breaking away from the societal institutions that hold Man back. Rather, it's a question of breaking away from industrial society's hierarchical thinking – the idea that success lies at the end of hard labor, and at the top rung of a ladder. This new Renaissance is the realization that we are all part of a great network, wherever we may be in time and physical place. It may even be the end of man's looking upon himself as a subject opposed to the world's objects – replaced instead by a mindset in which we consider ourselves all connected to one another. Those who grow up in this accelerated, hyper-integrated world will never fully understand that it was ever different. Their perception of the world will be that it is one big network where everything is connected and interpenetrating. Their way of consuming, socializing, philosophizing, working, communicating and loving is different. This makes them a different kind of human being than the human beings we have known before. Just as people before and after the Renaissance were very different from one another, there is a huge gap forming between Homo Industrialis and Homo Conexus. Once again, this book is written in an attempt to bridge that gap. One way of explaining how these type of societal changes can affect the value sets and behaviors of several generations, is the idea of *Cohort Theory.*

CHAPTER TWO:
ME AND MY COHORT

January 12, 1973 was quite an epic day for yours truly since this was the day I was born. But for everyone else but me, my mom, dad and some extended family, it was all about The King. Elvis Presley was on a stage in Hawaii. He was filming the rehearsals for his much anticipated concert, *Aloha From Hawaii*, which was to be beamed to the whole world via satellite a couple of days later. The concert, taped on January 12th, 1973, had two objectives: First, it was to be a run-through of the big event scheduled for two days later. Second, it was designed to provide the producers with broadcast-worthy content they could air in case something went wrong with the live satellite transmission. When the show aired two days later without a hitch, it was indeed a sensation. Satellite transmissions had been seen before – as with the pivotal broadcast of the lunar landing in 1969 – but this was the first time an *entertainment* event had been broadcast via satellite to the whole world.Forty million people from Asia and Europe watched while Elvis performed what many consider the final memorable concert before his tragic decline, which culminated in the infamous accidental overdose on his toilet in 1977. (US viewers didn't get to experience the show until three months later, as the Dolphins were playing the Redskins in Superbowl VII on the day of the concert.) The fact that I was born around the same time entertainment went global has – in a very real way – defined my life. I belong to the Television Generation, let's call us the TVG. The TVG'ers were the first to have that square wonder-box for a nanny, whenever mom and dad were too busy.

The generation born in the 1970s has never known a world without TV. And so for us, television became the Undisputed

Authority. While our parents' generation won't believe anything until it has been printed in a newspaper, for us a truth isn't a truth until some talking head has spoken it on TV. In the minds of all TVG-ers, human history before television invaded our living rooms seems quaint, unevolved, backwards. Not to be taken seriously. To the TVG, history started and ended with TV. As a kid growing up in Europe, it was in no way surprising or impressive that the 1982 Soccer World Cup from Spain was transmitted live via satellite to our homes. By then it was just a given.

The World's First Online Convergence Medium?

In Europe. they have something called *Teletext*. It's a thirty-year old technology that many people thought would die away when the Internet got out to the masses in the mid-nineties. Turns out Teletext was a little more resilient than that. But the fact that this old, primitive information technology is still alive today is not the real issue here. It's what it meant to those who grew up in Northern Europe in the 80s that makes it essential to understanding the Network Society and Homo Conexus. Teletext primed a whole generation for the coming of the Internet age. Even though several attempts were made, Teletext never made it big in the U.S. But in Europe, and particularly in Scandinavia, it really exploded when it was introduced in the early 80s. It is basically a catalogue of text pages you can read off your TV. Sort of a whole screen filled with browsable digital text, resembling closed captioning, just all over the screen. To work it, you pressed the special Teletext button on your remote, which switched the TV into text mode (Meanwhile, the sound of whatever show you were watching was still playing in the background.) Onto the screen would pop a Table Of Contents with world news, TV listings, sports scores, weather reports and other relevant stuff, next to a three-digit number. To view that page's contents, you simply punched in the appropriate three-digit number on your remote. The content was useful. But by today's – or even yesterday's – standards, the graphics were truly terrible. Think first generation Atari gaming console circa 1981 – and all text. But it worked like a charm. You'd get the information you wanted right away. In the U.S., a Teletext-styled system called *Electra* ran from 1980 to 1993, but if you didn't have a television set produced by Zenith, you couldn't use it. Other local televsion-based texting services sprang up, like *Metrotext* from KTTV in Los Angeles, and a few other fledgling initiatives. But TV text pages never really took off in the States as they did in Europe. I clearly remember the day in 1983, when my childhood friend Flemming came over to tell me that his family had just bought a new television, and that it was a pretty tricked-out one. Whenever someone bought a new TV in those days, it was a big deal. Even so, Flemming's family's new TV was extra special. Not only did it have stereophonic sound (wow!), it had Teletext. When I first saw Teletext at Flemming's house, I thought my head would explode. As a big science-fiction fan, it was a mind-blowing experience to see that here and now – in the non-fiction world – it was possible to retrieve information, and to go rummaging around, page by page, through an entire universe of topics. This was the first time I had felt any sense of command over what took place on the TV screen. It was on-demand information which was being updated frequently. It wasn't the news on the radio or TV, for which you had to wait until the proper time. It wasn't the morning paper, which would already be outdated by afternoon. The thought of being able to pull information up on your TV screen, at will – information that was constantly being refreshed – was a revolution to us in the Television Generation. For some of us it was an early glimpse of an interconnected network society in a not too distant future. It was my first taste of what it feels like to be online. *Connected!*

Nothing would ever be the same again.

Even today 2.5 million people a week in my native Denmark (half the population!) still use Teletext, which makes it one of the biggest – if not *the* biggest – news media in the country. In countries like The Netherlands, Germany, France and the U.K.

this 30-year-old technology is still being used by a substantial amount of people – *including kids.* This remains true even after the flourishing of the internet and the EPGs of the digital television era. The fact that I, and my peers from the Television Generation, can remember the very moment when Teletext appeared, makes quite a statement. It was the proverbial "line drawn in the sand," after which our lives began lurching in a whole new direction. Things would never be the same. It was a life-changing lightning bolt. The advent of Teletext remains a vivid memory, taking center stage in my tale of myself, just at the time when my identity was beginning to experience major changes.

The BBC's version of Teletext is called Ceefax, here showing some soccer results on a tube TV. It was launched in 1974 and expexted to run at least until 2012.

Obviously, I don't personally remember the *Aloha From Hawaii* concert. But I've always taken the idea of satellite broadcasts for granted, just as both my parents and I take electricity for granted. Can you actually envision a life without running water? To me now, it all feels as if daily life was never any different. And yet, Teletext and the internet are things that came into being only in my own lifetime. When Teletext flashed into my life, I was only 10 years old. In 1995, the web and e-mail invaded my life, and once again my mind got blown. By the '90s, mobile phones were something most people could afford, and wanted to spend money on. Imagine all those 90s kids, becoming socially aware in the world we know today.

Today's 10-somethings can't imagine life without the internet, cellular phones, file sharing and social networks, just as I can't imagine life without satellite TV transmissions. Even their older siblings, who came of age around 2009, feel this way. Because for anyone born in 1991, it was to be only be four years until the internet's explosive breakthrough in the Western world. Unless you're talking to someone with a preternaturally keen memory, they can only vaguely recall Mom and Dad bringing the first modem into the household. Or when they saw a cell phone for the first time. The Network Generation takes the internet and cell phones for granted, in the same way satellite transmissions are taken for granted by the Television Generation. Much like a kid who was born on the day Elvis rehearsed for his *Aloha from Hawaii* show. The appearance of Teletext, along with the later emergence of the personal computer, were such defining moments for us. These moments played a major role in shaping us as during our formative years, and tell us something about how we will act for the rest of our lives. The science behind these thoughts is called Cohort Theory. And it becomes particularly interesting when we look at the generations to whom the arrival of the internet and cellular phones are defining moments.

A Beginner's Guide To Cohort Theory

In their landmark book *Defining Markets, Defining Moments,* Geoffrey Meredith, Charles Schewe and Janice Karlovich describe how targeted consumers in different markets are shaped and colored by defining moments in their lives. The authors conclude that modern marketing must be more precise. To make a message resonate with any given target audience, you need to understand them better. How so? They write:

"Our approach focuses on the idea that to develop a rapport with, and understanding of, your customers, you must tap into the latent feelings and values formed when they were coming of age, a time that for most of us falls roughly between the ages of 17 and 23. While in this age span, your customers likely fell in love for the first time, became economic beings, developed their own value systems, explored new ideas, and, essentially became adults. "Coming of age" is a very powerful time, and the values that are instilled then last a lifetime. We use the term "generational cohort" to refer to groups of people who went through this important stage at roughly the same time."

There's another way of saying this. If the reasoning in *Defining Markets, Defining Moments* is right – that life-values in America are defined between ages 17 and 23 – then that definition probably happens a little earlier to Europeans. Europe has a more liberal attitude towards young people exploring limits, and this impacts their subsequent self-definition. One example is the legal age at which young people are allowed to buy and use alcohol. In Europe it is between 15 and 18, while, it's 21 all across the United States. But for the sake of argument, let's accept the age-limits presented in the book. It's been roughly 16 years since the internet became central to our lives. This was in 1995, just as the cellular phone blossomed as a gadget that everyone simply had to have. This means we have had 16 years' worth of a Network Cohort consisting of 17- 23-year-olds. Upper end members of this cohort were born as far back as

1972. (or 1973, the year Elvis sang to the world via satellite.) This explains why we can't just define the Homo Conexus group as consisting of teens or young adults. Homo Conexus'es are closing in on their forties – and then we aren't even counting the ones that are older, and who are taking on the Homo Conexus lifestyle. However, it is evident that young people today are shaped by the fact that they have never known a world without vast networking possibilities. It carves their identities out of networks they inhabit. In the October 2001 edition of *On The Horizon* (MCB University Press, October 2001), writer and e-learning specialist Marc Prensky published *Digital Natives, Digital Immigrants*. He describes the difference between Digital Natives – who have never known a world without internet and cell phones – and Digital Immigrants, who are recent arrivals in a world where they can barely speak the digital language. He doesn't specify which birth years qualify someone as a Digital Native. But he does stress that the term pretty much describes his present students, who are about to leave college. American colleges generally graduate students around age 22 or 23 . So, since the article was written in 2001, we may assume that Prensky thinks you should be from around 1978 to be a part of Generation "N," "D," "Y" or "Z," as this cohort is also called. Allowing a variable of 5 or 6 years to accommodate national and international differences in human maturation, the group would also include those born in the early 1970s. The difference is that *not everyone born in the 1970s is by nature a Connected Human*. On the other hand, practically all people born after 1990 *are* Connected Humans. And the older network people are, the fewer network peers they are likely to have who are their own age. This, as mentioned earlier, makes the Homo Conexus cohort quite a diverse crowd, not tied by numerical age, but rather by inherent values, social patterns and mindset. And – as we shall see in upcoming chapters – time and place are notions that are partly dissolved in the Homo Conexus perception of the world.

CHAPTER THREE:
HOMO CONEXUS IS BORN

Giant developmental leaps, like the transition from Industrial Man to Homo Conexus, don't take place overnight. Nor overweek. Not even overyear.

Paradigm shifts take time to sink into a culture.

After Gutenberg invented moveable type – ultimately enabling everyone to educate themselves – it still took many decades for what we might call "Renaissance Man" to blossom. Homo Conexus has been equally long in the making. The social conditions that promote "connectivism" date way back to the mid-18th Century. The technological breakthroughs that led to the emergence of this new type of human being, started back in the 19th century. And by the end of the 20th Century, a constellation of technologies, scientific research, cultural phenomena and events combined to bring the ideal of an interconnected society to reality. Clearly, in spite of what of some "experts" would say, it wasn't just the introduction of the internet that set the stage for Homo Conexus. Cell phones and other hand-held social media technologies are just as important as the internet in this regard. Other factors include satellite TV, the development and affordability of personal computers and other private technologies, the fall of the Berlin Wall and other constituents of what we call globalization. All of these elements are interrelated. If we look upon this network of factors and events, we get a bird's eye view that explains why *now* is the time that Homo Conexus is finally ready to meet the world.

In this chapter and the ones that follow, we take a closer look at these factors. Why is understanding globalization so crucial to the understanding of Homo Conexus? What would have happened if it had never become natural to own a personal computer? And not least – what has the mobile phone contributed to our sense of self? It's important to recognize the social progression that gave birth to Homo Conexus. From cohort theory we've learned that defining moments can impact the identity of a whole generation. Now let's look closer at those defining moments that gave birth to Homo Conexus.

The (Auto)Mobile Phone

There's a reason a Finnish company, Nokia, has become the largest mobile phone producer in the world. The mobile phone was born in Scandinavia. Before the multipurpose portable command centers we all carry in our pockets today, the mobile phone was primarily something that belonged in a car. Hence the term. The initial reason for this was that the battery and the transmitter were so large, that one needed a trunk for the transportation of them. The car's battery was needed to power the phone. The first models were tied into a central switchboard. You dialed in to the switchboard, which then forwarded your call. There were few channels to choose from, and sometimes you could hear other conversations underneath your own. The traffic was analog, not digitally encrypted as it is today. This basically means you could buy a radio frequency scanner and tune in to car phone frequencies if you wanted to eavesdrop on conversations. It's a good thing that such talk rarely dealt with matters of national security, but mostly about appointment schedules, pizza orders and notice that you were running late due to hassles with traffic. Children of the 1970s saw this same phenomenon growing up, roughly around the same time that Teletext and the PC entered our lives.

My father was sales manager for a construction machinery company. As such he was an early bird when it came to car phones, having his installed in 1983. Two years later, he was one of only 110,000 Scandinavians who had a phone in their car. As with Teletext, which provided constantly updated, on-demand information, it was mind-blowing to be able to connect with the entire world, from anywhere at all – even if you did have to do it from your car, and the connection had all the audio fidelity of a World War II-vintage walkie-talkie. In fact, it wasn't long after World War II that mobile phone technology came into existence. The first car phone conversation took place on December 3rd, 1950. Sture Lauhrén, a 37-year old engineer picked up the phone as he was driving peacefully along the Vasavägen in Stockholmin a van belonging to the national, Swedish telecommunications provider *Televerket*. It was only a "time check" service on the other end of the call, but still Lauhrén was excited. That simple phone call was the result of many years of preparation successfully put to the test. It was a great moment when he actually succeeded in getting through. The phone, battery, transmitter and accessories weighed 88 pounds in all. Not a device you'd be likely to clip on your belt or slip into your purse. But it was a start. It was another five years before the first fully automatic mobile phone system was offered for installation. However, that system only worked in Stockholm. Another major obstacle remained. In order to make a call, users needed direct radio contact with the central switchboard they were affiliated with. Today we can slip smoothly from one cell to another. ("Cell" is the technical term for the send/receive station – or antenna tower – that the phone connects to, and by extension, the area it covers.) But at that time it wasn't possible to hand a call from one cell to another. If you lost radio contact with your cell, well, *oops!* Too bad. The call ended. There was only one cell in Stockholm at the time, so it really didn't matter. In 1956 another cell was established in Gothenburg. That meant that Lauhrén's system (called *MTA, Mobile Telephone System A*) now served – hold on – a grand total of 19 mobile phones in Stockholm and 8 in Gothenburg! Up through the 1960s and 1970s the cells gradually grew in number, the phones themselves become smaller, and the idea of mobile phones gained wider acceptance. In the early 1980s, *NMT* introduced the first pan-Nordic system with reliable, smooth handover, available to all.[1]Meanwhile, in the U.S., Bell Laboratories had been working on mobile phone theory since 1947, and were, among other things, working on what we call the *distributed principle*. This meant that, instead of one broadcast mast in the middle of the cell (or transmission area), more masts were placed in a hexagonal array, one in each corner. For successful voice transmission, the masts had to be able to send and transmit in three different directions simultaneously (a principle which is still in effect). The only problem was that in those days it wasn't possible to do in the real world. Although the theory worked perfectly well on paper, the technology hadn't been invented yet. Further, the U.S. telecommunications authorities had not yet permitted use of the necessary frequencies. And as the Cold War escalated throughout the 1950s, the Americans moved their focus away from the civilian telephone market and concentrated on military communications instead. When the Soviet Union took the lead in the space race by launching Sputnik in 1957, President Eisenhower and his (somewhat stunned and embarrassed) administration reacted with a list of new initiatives to bolster the U.S. defense posture. One of these was the ARPA (*Advanced*

---

[1] Mobile phone technology was also being developed in the Soviet Union. In 1957, Leonid Kupriyanovich came up with the *LK-1*, a mobile phone which could be comfortably carried about by a person. The *LK-1* (Leonid's initials – coincidence?) wasn't perfect by our standard. But it was a step forward. Weighing in at "only" 6.6 lbs, it had an effective reach of 30 meters – just under 100 feet – with far more battery power than most other models then in service. He followed up with a pocket model in 1958 which weighed just over one pound.

That same year, the USSR launched a national campaign to give civilians access to mobile phone technology. In 1963 the *Altay* system was introduced in Moscow. By 1970 it had spread to 30 cities across the Soviet Union, but due to wariness on both sides of the Iron Curtain, the technology never reached the rest of the world.

Research Project Agency), which was to become the nesting ground for the internet. ARPA had a budget for offering development-deals to many private companies in the U.S., and consequently it became more lucrative for the technology businesses to develop things of military relevance rather than, for instance, private mobile phone technology. For this reason, the development of mobile phone technology was put on hold in the U.S. until well into the 1960s, by which time Scandinavia and Japan had already staked out a technological and market-oriented approach, which gave both regions a head start they have maintained to this day.

The Mobile Phone Without The (Auto)Mobile

What made mobile technology truly mobile was when the U.S. got back in the game. This can be accredited to Amos E. Joel, Jr., an engineer with Bell Labs – the company that had worked with mobile phone technology since just after World War II. In 1970, Joel discovered how to do an automatic handover of a mobile phone from one cell to the next. This rebooted the American development of mobile phone technology. In 1971 AT&T, the owner of Bell Labs, started a long campaign to get the government to reserve certain frequencies for civilian mobile phone use. It would take 11 years before the Federal Communications Commission finally granted permission in 1982. Not that the business community didn't try to influence the outcome by lobbying and PR campaigns. Motorola had long been a key player in American radio communications. Their products were immensely popular: walkie-talkies; two-way radios for truckers and equipment for amateur radio operators. They now entered the battle to put mobile phone technology on the agenda. And on April 3rd, 1973 Motorola's Dr. Martin Cooper went out into a New York City street, followed by the media, and called Dr. Joel Engel, his rival and friend, a driving force behind Bell's mobile phone research. This is recorded as the first-ever phone call from a handheld mobile telephone. And it took place only a few months after Elvis said *Aloha from Hawaii*. Cooper called from a prototype of Motorola's *Dynatac* phone, later dubbed "The Brick" for obvious reasons. That's right. It really looked like a brick. But what was fantastic about this incredibly expensive prototype was that it was *handheld*. You didn't need a monster battery in your car to make it work. You could stick it in your briefcase, even in the pocket of your overcoat. Almost 20 years were to pass before this prototype could be used on a greater network. By then, production had become so reasonably priced that the average man on the street could afford one. [2]

The *DynaTAC 8000X* phone, which Dr. Martin Cooper had demonstrated to a gaggle of curious reporters, was approved by

---

2

In 1971 Finland launched the first successful commercial cell phone network, called *ARP* (the appropriate acronym for *AutoRadioPuhelin*, Finnish for "auto radio phone"). The Finnish head start – one part of the generalized Scandinavian head start – would soon supercharge the country's economy. Even at this writing, the Finnish company Nokia remains the world's largest producer of mobile phone technology.

The Japanese were also at work on mobile telephony. The national phone company *NTT* (*Nippon Telegraph and Telephone*), doing business as the privatized *NTT Docomo*, introduced Japan's first mobile phone service in 1979. By that time the *ARP* network in Finland had already reached full geographic coverage. So even though the Japanese often claim to have launched the first publicly accessible cell phone network, the Finns beat them by 8 years. As early as 1977, while *NTT* was just building its network, *ARP* already had some 10,000 subscribers.

The tiny island state of Bahrain, tucked away in the Persian Gulf, was also in the game. In fact, they opened their public mobile phone service in 1978, a year before the Japanese.
From around 1980 on, there was no turning back. Mobile phones were on the march. Trunk loaded car phones came first. Next came mobile phones you could use away from the car, but which were still too big to be conveniently portable. Both hands were needed to operate them, so it could hardly be called a handset.

the FCC in 1983. So the following year, yuppies could impress friends and girlfriends by talking on the phone... anytime, anywhere. As long as they stayed in big cities – the only places which carried a signal. The use of this fancy, handheld model was still basically reserved for the affluent. But over the course of the 80s and 90s, the use of a variety of models of both car and mobile phones became more widespread.

My Very Own Brick

The *DynaTAC* was a tough little devil, still in production 20 years after its creation. The European version became my own first cell phone. My friend Lars and I had shared a great passion for technology ever since we were schoolboys. And when he showed me his brand new mobile phone in 1994, I revisited that mind-blowing sensation of 11 years earlier, when I talked to my mom on my dad's car phone and experienced Teletext for the first time. I knew that my world had been expanded. Again.

Naturally I had heard of and seen cell phones. But I had never held one in my hand. Lars's little beauty was the *Motorola DynaTAC International 3200*. It was the redesigned *GSM* version of the phone, introduced to the American market 10 years earlier. It was still *The Brick*, and it was still very heavy. But who cared? It was way cool! Luckily for me, Lars soon tired of it. So I inherited it when he switched to the lighter, more modern *Nokia 2010* in 1995 – the first Nokia to reach the masses. And when Lars showed me how to send little text messages to other cell phones, I was completely won over. My world had changed completely – even if the only other person I could text message was Lars. Between 1995 and 1996 I went through four different cell phones – symptomatic of the way Homo Conexus would later perceive technology: as something that was – *and ought to be* – constantly changing. I went on to take over Lars's Nokia 2010 when he bought his Nokia 2110, the first big cell phone "hit." For its time, it had an exclusive design and was diminutively sized. And it had an antenna that could be pulled out and pushed back in. Then, into my life in quick succession, came the *Motorola StarTAC* which looked like a car when the cover was shut, and it was put down on the table. Soon after that, an Alcatel, an Ericsson, another Nokia, an Ericsson again, Nokia again, then a Sony Ericsson – and so forth. While this was happening in my own phone-life, more and more people were getting cell phones. So now we could call or text message one another at any hour of the day. And believe me, we did. Old telephone culture was replaced by new. As the number of people with Caller ID mushroomed, we stopped presenting ourselves when calling someone – because we knew they could see who was calling. And when answering, we'd start right out with by just saying the person's name, or simply "What's up?" because *we* knew who was calling *us*. After years of mobile phoning, it was dawning on people how many habits had changed from the *Age Of The Land Lines*. One of the things that sets Homo Conexus apart from Industrial Man is that telecommunication has become individualized. During the *Age Of The Land Lines*, when the telephone rang, it was common to try to predict who was calling. ("You answer it, it's probably for you.") There was a time when everyone in your household was on the same line. You might pick up the phone in the den, and hear your sister talking on the extension in her room, and she'd quickly bark at you to get off the line – *now!* That seems absurd today, when our telecommunications are overwhelmingly private. But in those days, the land line was the *de facto* central that everyone in the house had to share when they wanted to communicate. Today we interconnect one on one the vast majority of the time. As noted above, it has become *individualized*. This is emblematic of the sea-change from the Industrial Society's centralized way of thinking, to the Network Society's de-centralized mindset. The Beatles' classic line "Honey, disconnect the phone" from *Back in the U.S.S.R.* doesn't make sense anymore. Nothing is plugged in any more. And the call making procedure is physically different. I now have difficulties calling from a landline. Because I'm so used to dialing the number and *then* hitting the call button, it's unusual for me to dial the number and then ... *wait.* It's as if something is missing. Are you old enough to remember when you carried a little phone book around with you? Or a list of important numbers on a slip of paper in your wallet? When was the last time you "let your fingers do the walking" in the White Pages? Homo Conexus would have no idea what you were talking about, if you asked them to do that little exercise. And what about all those numbers you once knew by heart? How many do you know today? In that area at least, we aren't exercising our brain capacity any more. We'd rather use that capacity for something else, because all the numbers we need are already programmed into our phones – or easily accessible from the internet directly to the phone. The youngest members of the Homo Conexus species, the so-called *Digital Natives* , have never experienced the abovementioned things. To them, a phone number is something you get once, then punch into your phone's memory ... then forget about. Now the phone knows it, it's no longer your problem! Further, it's no big deal when you want to change your phone service provider. You know there's always some better or cheaper service, with a newer, fancier phone attached to it. How Homo Conexus uses communication media – especially mobile phone technology – is something I will cover more fully in Chapter Eight. Right now, however, it's time to take a look at the other revolution that made the world ready for Homo Conexus: *the internet*.

Meeting The Maker

Paul Baran was already standing in the doorway when I pulled into his driveway. He looked exactly as I had expected – only without glasses. An elderly gentleman (born in 1926 in what is now Belarus) standing beneath the warm California sun wearing a blue sports jacket, light pants and a stylish shirt. Baran lives in the idyllic area of Atherton, not far from Silicon Valley. It's one of the most affluent and charming areas of the U.S., and it's easy to understand why he lives here. Because he was the first to design its structure, Paul Baran is among a handful of people who can legitimately say that they invented the internet. And although he wasn't involved in its subsequent technical development, many physicists agree that he, more than anyone, is the Father Of The Internet. Upon earning his Master's Degree in Engineering from UCLA in 1959, Baran went to work for the RAND Corporation, a private think tank and research organization, whose biggest client at the time was the U.S. Department of Defense (DOD). Baran already had broad experience with the military. He had worked for the Hughes Corporation for four years while finishing his degree. Hughes was a defense contractor for a private company commissioned to deliver "solutions" to DOD. Baran was one of the brains assigned to development of the nuclear ICBM "Minute Man" project. Even more importantly, along with his guided missile experience, he gained insight into network technology working on the SAGE (*Semi Automated Ground Environment*) guidance system, implemented by a network of radar stations all across the U.S. Does the expression "rocket science" ring a bell? This kind, gently aging genius got into my car, and we headed off to a local restaurant to do the interview over lunch. He looked like the man I had seen in the pictures from his days at RAND, only now he seemed not to need the heavy glasses he wore at the time. His hair had turned gray, nearly white. Like a grandfather telling his grandson about the Good Old Days, he recounted how he became the first of many souls whose combined effort created the internet – the internet that has become so central to our lives, the aorta in the heart of Homo Conexus. The internet we have so quickly come to take for granted. The roots of the internet go deep into the nuclear arms race between the U.S. and the USSR in the 1950s. As Baran remembers it:

"I got into this by a very curious path. The big issue at the time was strategic command and control communication. I joined the RAND Corporation, which is set up to work in the national security area…it was set up during World War II to preserve the operational capability that the Air Force had developed. It has since gone on to doing many other things, but at the time, the cold war tension between the U.S. and the USSR was extremely great. Both sides were building nuclear weapons and their

delivery systems, and there was a realization, that whichever side went first would probably destroy the other country. So there was a tremendous fear of somebody going off unilaterally. That was the environment at the time, and there was a realization that even if somebody fired their weapons just to destroy the other guys' weapons, say the U.S., the receiving party, that the collateral damage would take out the telephone system. And a single high altitude nuclear burst would take out all high frequency communication, so then there would be no communication to control the weapons."

Baran made it clear to me that his primary goal was to work on communication paths during wartime when phone lines and high frequency radio communications were threatened.

"The problem with the telephone system falling apart was the switching centers. There weren't very many, we tended to build highly centralized systems, and just knocking out a few of the major centers took everything out."

It is often said that the internet was created by the U.S. Department Of Defense for military purposes. This isn't 100% correct. Even though the DOD funded initiatives that would eventually lead to the creation the internet, it was ultimately in academia that the internet first saw the light of day. But it *was* in connection with Paul Baran's efforts to solve the problems with a vulnerable communication system, that he hit on something that would change the world forever.

"So would it be possible to build the network differently, distributed, sort of a fishnet? I examined this one, and found that as you increased the number of links, you got to a redundancy of about two and a half or three to one. In other words, two and half as many links as you needed just to connect the system together in that fashion. Then an interesting phenomenon took place, where the system became very robust. And you could chop it up

and make pieces that survived with a very high probability of being able to see one another."

So Baran's great discovery was that, by increasing the level of the links in the network, and thereby decreasing the importance of central hubs, a sturdiness emerged that spread to the rest of the network. The network became one connected entity, where the sum of its parts was as important as the individual parts. Now this finding was to be applied to everyday use. And for everyday use, it was necessary to have more of everything.

"I started adding up all the communication required, and turned the problem around. I tried to give 'em so much communication that it would be equal to or more than they had at the time."

While Baran was working on this abundance of communication paths, a new idea entered his mind, which also occurred to two other researchers at about the same time, independent of Paul Baran's work. This new idea is now seen as fundamental to the modern network idea. It is essential to how the internet works, how cell phones work, even how networks within our bodies' cells function.

It's all about packets.

Good things come in small packets

Baran's objective in creating his "sturdy" network (where parts could be lost without the system itself being lost) was to create a way for a message to always have an alternative routing possibility. In other words, if a message hit a dead-end anywhere on its way through the system, there would be another "escape route" to the recipient.

"We knew it would not be possible to synchronize each of these links. We had to do it asynchronous. The only way to do that was to break everything up into very small packets, all of the same size, and treat each packet as a separate message with enough intelligence for it to find its way through the network. So the idea was really based on the inability to synchronize a network like that. And then we said, well if you do that then every link could run at its own speed, which mean we could keep a lot of facilities in place. So that's where the idea came from...the necessity of packets."

The idea of a distributed network of "packets," separate discrete elements combining to create one message at the end, was inspired by Warren McCulloch, one of Baran's friends. He was doing research on how the brain processes messages. By discovering neural networks, he helped start what we now think of as the cybernetic movement. More on this in Chapter Four, when we look into the working of body networks. The idea of "packets" went by different names, and as a matter of fact, Baran's definition didn't end up being the generally accepted one.

"I called them message blocks, and about 5 years later, Donald Davies independently came up with the same idea, and he called them packets, and the word "packet" was a much better choice for words. "

Donald Davies (1924-2000) was a Welsh scientist who began working for the British *National Physical Laboratory* in 1947. He was part of a small team anchored by the brilliant English computer legend Alan Turing, who revolutionized computer programming. Turing was building a computer system called *ACE* for the British government. Davies joined the team, and later on headed a program to apportion government funding to the British computer industry. Around this time he conceived the notion of *packet switching* Baran mentions in the quote above. Packet switching is the same principle as the one Baran discusses, a message is split into little "packets" that are sent asynchronously out into the network, but which then pool into one big packet upon reaching the recipient. Baran had described the principle to RAND between 1960 and 1962, and these ideas ultimately emerged in a proposal for implementation in 1964. The reason Baran prefers Donald Davies's term *packet switching*, even though this wasn't introduced until 1965, is because *packets* is more efficient term for something being sent; with a sender, a recipient and a time-designation "stamped" on it. Modern day computers on the network can easily repair any mistakes in the communication routes, thereby ensuring a stable flow on the internet. But it wasn't always like that, explains Baran:

"At the time, we didn't have enough computer power to do error correction, but error detection was easy, so that's why we went to a cyclical redundancy test. In the packet, we'd have a "to-address" and a "from-address," now we needed a measure for how long the packet flowed in the network - a time stamp. So we chose to use how many times you'd relayed it. It would give the receiving end an idea of where the messages came from and how to send messages to that spot. With the error checking out of the way, we kept a carbon copy of whatever we sent, and that made it feasible to operate with unreliable links. Cause if something went wrong, you could just resend the packet."

Baran's work laid the foundation for the way the internet, and all other digital networks, would eventually function. He is the genius behind the concept of sending messages as tiny individual packets that scurry through the network, re-assembling only when they reach the recipient. Perhaps most inspiring is Baran's prescient distinction between three different types of networks: centralized, de-centralized and distributed. These three types of networks had never been conveyed as clearly as when Baran described them. His models made it dazzlingly clear that networks aren't just networks – and that there is a difference between centralizing and de-centralizing in a network.

And that centralized networks were not the future.

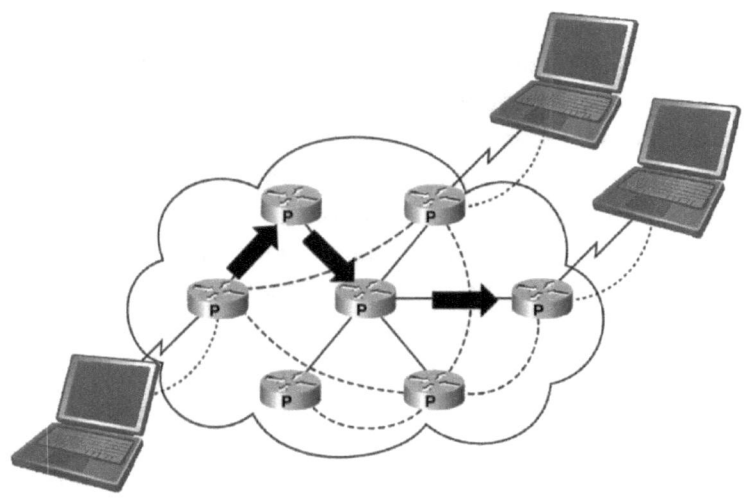

How a packet finds its own way through the network.

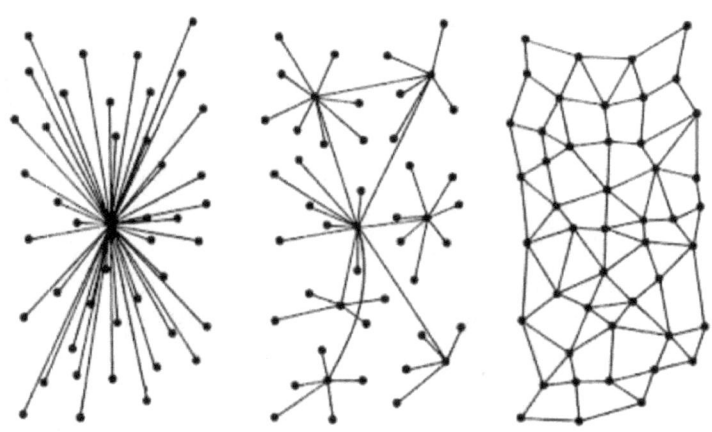

Centralized   De-centralized   Distributed

Baran's models for networks: the centralized, the de-centralized, and the distributed network

This is probably Paul Barans's greatest gift to the world. With his scientific proof that a decentralized world is more robust and safe than a world where everything depends on just a few centers, he predicted one of the most important megatrends of the last 100 years – that of decentralization. (More on this later.) Roughly at the same time Paul Baran was laboring away at RAND exploring relationships among increased linkage levels and network sturdiness, a young man named Leonard Kleinrock was finishing his Ph.D. thesis at the Massachusetts Institute of Technology (MIT). Dr. Leonard Kleinrock hasn't lost his thick New York accent, although he left the East Coast in the mid-sixties. After finishing his doctorate, Kleinrock accepted an offer to teach at the University of California at Los Angeles (UCLA), where he later became a professor. And UCLA was where he did his part to get the internet into gear.

Meeting The Maker, Part II

When I went to see him in his little book filled office at UCLA, the IMP was outside the door. IMP is short for *Interface Message Processor* and is really just a modem, but with a router the size of a wardrobe closet. This piece of technology didn't do anything except pass data along, but that was pretty impressive stuff back in 1969, when Kleinrock had it delivered to his office. This was the machine which would be the hook-up – the translator – between the two machines that would be connected on October 29th, 1969, and hereby become the first two computers on the ARPAnet - which later would become the internet. Kleinrock became a part of the creation of the internet almost as haphazardly as Baran. If he hadn't had a good friend by the name of Larry Roberts he might have been relegated to the status of a minor character – just a footnote figure – in internet history.

"[The network didn't get started] until ARPA came along and decided they wanted to build a network, and they put Larry Roberts in charge of making that happen, and he and I were

office mates at MIT, so he knew exactly what I'd done, so he brought me in, and I helped him specify what the network would be…and UCLA, where I was now a Professor, was selected to be the first node on the network."

As mentioned before, it is a common misconception that the internet was conceived by the American military. And it's easy to arrive at that misconception. ARPA is short for *Advanced Research Project Agency,* which was a department under the U.S. Department of Defense at the Pentagon. ARPA (as mentioned earlier) was commissioned by President Eisenhower in 1957 after the Russians had won the race to conquer space by launching the Sputnik satellite. Eisenhower wanted to use his military budget to develop new technologies that everyone could benefit from. Since then the department has had "D" for "defense" added to the beginning of the acronym. Today, DARPA works primarily to develop advanced weapons for the military. And had it not been for Bob Taylor, who worked at ARPA at the time, the work of Baran and Kleinrock would never have gotten past the planning stages. Bob Taylor was administrating a part of the research funds that ARPA would dole out to different labs. To keep score with what was going on with the different projects, he had three different terminals hooked up to three different, larger computer systems that were off-site. As time progressed, Taylor got increasingly frustrated that he had to consult three different computers – *why couldn't all the computers just talk to each other?* So he went up to his boss and asked for a million dollars. Which he got in 20 minutes. Taylor's boss could easily see the genius in having different computers talk to each other across a network. It was Taylor who then hired Larry Roberts, who then in turn hired Kleinrock and made sure that UCLA and Stanford became the two first nodes on the ARPAnet – and thereby the internet. Even though ARPA was paying, there wasn't much Pentagon involvement in the development of the internet. The universities took over immediately, since they needed more processing power for the math calculations in their research. At the time there was only one computer at every university, so the thought of connecting them to combine their power was alluring. It would theoretically be possible to perform the calculations much faster, and also to make more calculations with such a hookup. This was the real driving force behind the creation of the internet: the ability to share data and processing power. As we will see later, sharing became a driving force in the network society. From 1964 through 1968 Bob Taylor, Larry Roberts, Leonard Kleinrock and a slew of other bright researchers on both the East and West Coasts, collaborated in hammering out a workable theory of the internet. One of the stories Leonard Kleinrock loves to tell is the one about the day the internet was "born" – the day when two computers were first connected via a telephone network. Many events that fundamentally change the world start out unnoticed – this was also the case with the internet.

"Out of my laboratory, we sent the very first message, on October 29th, 1969. The first message went from my laboratory to the second node in the network up at Stanford Research Institute. The first message was "LO". We didn't plan it that way, we didn't have a good message, but accidentally, we sent only LO of a LOGIN message. It was a wonderful message, 'cause it predicted: "Lo and behold", what better message could you have? Short and prophetic. We wanted a LOGIN from our host computer to the other host on the network, which was the Stanford Research Institute host. And in order to do that, you type in "L,O,G" and the machine up at Stanford had the ability to basically complete commands, so if it sees you type LOG it will type the IN for you, because there's no other word that you could be typing. What you gotta do is type LOG. So we had my programmer, with a set pair of headphones talking to a programmer up there, a guy named Duvall, as well as the data network to communicate with. He sent the L and he said "You got the L?". The guy said "I got the L". He sent the O. "You got the O?" Got the O. Sent the G. "Got the G?"

CRASH!

The damn machine broke down. And it wasn't our host, it wasn't the network, it wasn't the switches or the line, it was the Stanford Research Institute host. So the first message was LO ... "

...says Leonard Kleinrock and laughs. When the internet saw the light of day for the first time – it also *crashed* for the first time, which has its own irony to it! When you think about how important this little incident in October 1969 would become, it is stunning that nobody thought anything of it.

"And you know, we didn't plan it, because we didn't have a good message like 'What had God roared' or 'A giant leap for mankind'. We didn't have a camera. We didn't have a microphone. There's no recording of that event. The only anticipation of what we were doing in published form was a press release that I put out months before that, four months before, in which I articulated what I thought this network would become."

Kleinrock is also keenly aware of the immense impact his creation has had on his fellow creatures. He thinks that technology ultimately plays only a minor part in the internet's influence on human progress. But he didn't realize the scale until 1971, when a programmer from BNN, Ray Tomlinson, invented a system for sending text messages through ARPAnet using the symbol @ as separator between the sender and the place, thereby inventing e-mail.

"The piece of the vision that I didn't have at that time was that my 97-year old mother would be on the internet today, and she is. I didn't see that it wasn't about computers talking to each other, it was about people interacting. Communities forming. Special interest communities. The first time I realized that was when, in 1972 e-mail was introduced to the network by Tomlinson – and it suddenly took over the traffic of the network. I said "Wow. What's going on?... Oh, it's about people communicating!"

Kleinrock had made certain predictions before the first router, built by BNN, landed at his office on August 29th, 1969. On July 3rd 1969, UCLA issued the aforementioned press release, stating that the university would be the first center in a large computer network. Kleinrock states that computer networks aren't a new phenomenon, pointing to SAGE (which Paul Baran had worked on), a network of military radar-stations; and SABRE, a computer-network used by the airlines for reservations. But these two systems were built with a specific purpose – the new network could be used to transmit any type of data via the telephone grid that everybody had access to.

At the end of the UCLA press release Kleinrock makes his most poetic statement:

"As of now, computer networks are still in their infancy," says Dr. Kleinrock, "But as they grow up and become more sophisticated, we will probably see the spread of 'computer utilities', which, like present electric and telephone utilities, will service individual homes and offices across the country."

That hot summer of July, 1969 in L.A., Dr. Kleinrock not only predicted the spread of personal computers, which 15 years later would be common household items, but also that those computers eventually would be connected to each other in an immeasurably huge network. But, as he now points out, he didn't foresee that the computer-network wasn't about computers, *but rather about human contact*. However, someone else did foresee that future. In 1968, Bob Taylor, along with his mentor and former boss, J.C.R. Licklider, wrote a paper called *The Computer as a Communications Device*, which pretty much foresaw everything we use the internet for today. From e-mails to online dating. From videochat to webshops. The men who secured the funding for the early internet documented their visions, 30 years before it became a reality. This happened, when Tim Berners-Lee at CERN in Switzerland invented a program and a set of protocols that used the internet to archive documents – and which suddenly mutated into the World Wide Web. An application which brought the internet to the masses. Later, the *www* was destined to evolve into such a useful tool for gathering data about networks that worldwide network structures were suddenly everywhere apparent. Suddenly we could see and study the networks themselves. This sequence of events paved the way for the emergence of an entirely new breed of Homo Sapiens: the Connected Human, Homo Conexus.

***

CHAPTER FOUR:
SECOND NATURE - THE
NETWORKS IN YOUR BODY

There seem to be networks everywhere these days – and I don't mean old fashioned broadcast networks.

The term "network" – in its expanded sense – first became commonly used in the 1990s, when the internet and cellular phones started to play a serious part in our lives. Today you don't have "friends in high places," like in the 1980s. Now you have personal networks. You don't have a phone line; you're part of a tele-network. In the U.S., Verizon no longer markets itself as a telephone company, but rather as *America's Most Reliable Network.* You no longer meet colleagues at trade meetings; you're all together in professional or business networks – and so forth. But are you aware that the place where you connect with the most networks is within your own body? That the internet's structure is inspired by the network in your brain? You may not have thought much about this because, like most people, you're too busy living and breathing. But when you go online with your laptop and log in to Facebook, check in to a venue on Foursquare or read the latest sports updates on your iPhone; and so forth, an incredible parallel process is taking place, interweaving your brain, your body and the various network systems that are built into your physical body. This idea is called *connectionism*, and in recent years it has gone beyond philosophical and psychological theory into hard research in the fields of biology and physics. Thanks to the aforementioned friend of Paul Baran's, Warren McCulloch, whom you will get to know more in the following pages, the networks of the internet and cell phones bear an interesting similarity to the inner workings of your brain. Later in this chapter we will also meet a woman who is part of a remarkable group of scientists who are mapping how the cells of the body are networking with each other. These scientists are looking for structures that are similar to e.g. the internet, to better predict how cell networks will act under certain circumstances. In other words, if the cell networks in your body work like known network structures (like the internet, or the way we organize ourselves socially) it may be possible to predict the patterns of changes in cells. This would be a great step forward, for example, in the battles against cancer and Parkinson's Disease. Much is expected of this research. But the parallels between the body and the internet didn't begin last week. This journey to understanding began as long ago as the end of the 18th Century; quickened its pace in the 19th Century; and really became interesting in the 1950s. In 1855 the British multi-scientist Herbert Spencer (1820-1903) published the first edition of *Principles of Psychology*, a work he would keep refining until his death. It is among the earliest connectionist works, which introduces terms such as "structure" and "systems," believed used for the first time in the context of the workings of the brain. (Spencer is also the father of the term "survival of the fittest.") And after studying Darwin's *Origin Of Species* he postulated parallels to human survival in modern society which he called "social Darwinism"). Many other thinkers of this era became aware of the connected nature of the brain's function, one of them being Sigmund Freud (1856-1939), who examined the idea in his 1895 work, *Project For A Scientific Psychology.*

This was also the moment when scientists first started talking seriously about neurons.

A Big Network Of Little Grey Cells

A *neuron* is the technical term for what we laymen call a *brain cell*. These are the cells in the brain and throughout the nervous system that work together to create your thoughts and emotions.

They interpret the input from your senses – as forwarded by messages from your eyes, ears, nose, mouth and sense of touch. They're helped in this by the *glial cells* (*glia* is Greek for *glue*), whose sole function is to sustain and protect neurons. Glial cells make sure that neurons do their job. It was the Spanish scientist Santiago Ramón y Cajal (1852-1934) who first presented the idea of neurons to the world. This work won him the Nobel Prize for Medicine in 1906. It is impressive to see how closely his ink drawings of the nervous system, with which he clarified his research, match modern illustrations of neural networks. How enlightening it is to peek into the brain and discover that there are things happening there that are strongly reminiscent of the internet! But actually, it's the other way around. The internet's network was inspired by the brain's network, and it came about almost by chance. Details later. Let's stick with the brain a little while longer. Neurons work together to create the thoughts, feelings and perceptions that communicate what your senses are telling you. This process is very much like what happens when you call someone from a cell phone. Here's how:

It used to be commonly held that the central nervous system consists of tiny nerve fibres. But Ramón y Cajal proposed that it really consists of *billions of gooey little grey cells called neurons*. He and his colleagues couldn't be sure whether these neurons were connected to each other or not. But they were there, all right. Unfortunately, the technology needed to study neurons closely wasn't available until later on in the 20th Century. But further research based on Ramón y Cajal's theories proved that neurons actually did interact. What is even more interesting: it's not just that they work together – but *how they work together* – that creates our thoughts, feelings and interpretations of information from our senses. Seen through a microscope, neurons appear to be communicating with each other. They have a body (the *soma*), which contains the cell's nucleus. This is where you find your DNA code and everything else that makes you who you are, look the way you look and predispose you to your palette of personal skills and attributes. The *soma* itself looks somewhat like a chestnut, with little spikes or tentacles. These spikes, or tentacles, are called *dendrites.* The cell's "sender" is the *axon,* which resembles a spidery antenna protruding from the *soma.* Whenever you think or feel something, it's because millions of neurons have started communicating with each other, firing off messages from one neuron's *axon* to another neuron's *dendrite.* These messages – untold billions of axon-dendrite transactions constantly sizzling through your body's networks – are important. They consist of a series of commands for the receiving neuron, which is how the neuron "decides" what to do. For instance, a baby smiles at you. Processing this incoming information, neurons begin shooting messages to other neurons, until millions of micro-orders merge to create a collective image. Your system feels an emotion that makes you smile back at the child. If this reminds you of packet switching, it's no coincidence. This neural system parallels the way that the internet and cell phones work. Imagine that your neurons are communicating via micro-tiny mobile phones. A transmitting neuron sends an electrical impulse along its sender, the axon. This corresponds to it dialing a number from its cell phone, trying to contact another neuron. When one neuron's axon and another neuron's dendrites get close to each other, and one neuron's axon is loaded with the aforementioned electric impulse, then the two can communicate.

Bzzzt. Bzzzzzzt. *Contact.*

This electro-chemical buzz happens through a "phone central" called the *synapse.* The synapse is the center between two neurons, like the digital central you pass through when trying to reach someone on the cell phone. But just dialing isn't fun – it's the conversation that matters, right? As in the case of the mobile phone, there is *no physical contact* between the neurons when they communicate. Instead there is a protein in the transmitting neuron which alters shape, and in turn causes lots of little containers to open up within the neuron. These little containers, or *vesicles,* contain the orders one neuron wants to send to another. The packet of orders is called the *neuro-transmitter* and, just like the message you try to deliver using your cell phone, the neuro-transmitter plays a central role in *brokering the conversation between neurons.* It is the neuro-transmitter that tells the recipient neuron what to do to help your mental process work as smoothly and elegantly as possible. But there's nothing more annoying than trying to get an important message through during a call with a bad connection. We all know that frustrating "Hello? Can you hear me?" which puts a stop to so many communications. Same thing with neurons. If neuro-transmitter packets aren't sent efficiently from one neuron to another, things go wrong in your brain. Parkinson's Disease is an example of a disease that stems from "poor connections" between neurons that are trying to send the neuro-transmitter *dopamine* to each other. Bad connections when trying to communicate the neuro-transmitter *seratonin* can lead to depression. So it isn't just in your everyday life that bad connections can cause trouble – this is also the case in your brain's internal network of neurons. As mentioned before, the "telephone exchange" where two neurons meet is called the *synapse.* But there is another way neurons can communicate, called the *nexus.* In this case, the surfaces of the two neurons *actually do touch*, thus creating a path for communication. In the telephone analogy this would correspond to a land line. But whether the neurons connect via landline or via wireless connection is not important. What is important is to understand that *they do connect*. And, when they do connect, it's thanks to a neural network that closely resembles the computer networks or mobile phone networks we use every day. They transmit many little commands which, via a network, become one big action. When these networks light up, our thoughts come alive. Feelings emerge. And input from our senses is being processed. Imagine all this intricate communications among those little gooey grey neurons, creating a vast internally-connected network. This is called a neural network, and it is what inspired both Herbert Spencer and Sigmund Freud.

The Internet Is A Brain. Well, Almost.

When neurons communicate via millions of independent neuro-transmitters that end up as one whole entity, it is the same as when packets are sent via the internet, ending up as one cohesive message. It's exactly the same process that the creators of the internet came up with in the 1950s and early 1960s. When Paul Baran described his three types of networks, he was greatly inspired by neural networks. And his idea of a distributed network, where messages were sent in little packets to be gathered at the receiving end, was directly inspired by neural networks. As he told me:

"A guy I knew back in the old days, Warren McCulloch, brain surgeon, engineer, would say: "Looking at the brain, each part of the brain has a different function. If one part is injured, the function moves over to another part. The function does not live in this particular part of the brain, but moves," Baran explained during our lunch in Atherton.

A great example of how the brain works like the internet – or rather, the other way around, is what happened to Terry Wallis. Wallis, a now 47-year old man living in the Ozarks of Arkansas, woke up on June 11, 2003, and looked around in a room he didn't recognize. He saw a nurse, and asked her who the other woman in the room was. He was told that it was his mother, who he couldn't recognize either. No wonder. His mother had gotten almost 20 years older since he last saw her.

In 1984, the then 19-year old Terry Wallis crashed his car by driving through a roadside rail and tumbling off a 25-foot bluff. Two other friends were riding in the car with him, one was killed, another, miraculously survived without a scratch. Wallis was paralyzed and entered a comatose state that would last almost 19 years. Wallis would just lie there, unresponsive. He wasn't brain dead – just comatose. Around the turn of the millennium, Wallis started to respond to people who tried to communicate with him through small grunts and by blinking his eyes. And in the early summer of 2003, he went from a minimally conscious state to full consciousness. What the doctors and researchers studying Wallis' case found to be the reason for his slow, but miraculous recovery, was exactly what McCulloch had told Paul Baran about. Wallis' brain had slowly – very slowly - reprogrammed itself, finding and building new neural pathways through the brain to send the messages it needed to send. Just like a packet can reroute itself as it passes through the internet. This idea of the brain "re-directing" functions to a new route, inspired Baran to imagine the telecommunications system that replaced America's centralized tele-network, as described in the previous chapter. Baran's discussions with McCulloch provided the foundation for the internet's basic structure. It was an important historic milestone. But it was not until the 1940s, when McCulloch began publishing more in-depth material on the subject, that the idea and the potential of neural networks gained wider credibility. McCulloch's work helped launch the cybernetics movement – the revolutionary idea of the merging of man and machine, which was overdramatized into the advent of *cyborgs* seen in films, cartoons and science-fiction novels. His first experiments stretch back to the early 1920s, when he was finishing his education. It was only in the years leading up to World War II that his work – and his personality – started attracting attention. And with good reason. He decided it was time for a luxurious full beard. Eventually, as McCulloch began to grey prematurely, he looked like an elderly wizard. And even though beards were hip in the 1950s and 1960s, in academia and elsewhere, McCulloch's long white beard made him really stand out among his fellow scientists. It was, however, during his stay at the Psychiatric Department at the University of Illinois, Chicago, that he published his most groundbreaking scientific papers. In 1943 he published *A Logical Calculus of the Ideas Immanent in Nervous Activity* together with his colleague, the logician Walter Pitts. Behind that obscure, technical title was the now widely accepted idea that neurons function in networks.

And the revolutionary thought that it would be possible to simulate these networks electronically.

Recreation of neural activity in an artificial environment.

McCulloch and Pitts thought it possible to create a computer that behaved like a human brain by making it reach networked conclusions, rather than conclusions from a linear array of calculations. When Pitts and McCulloch published their results, the timing coincided excellently with the publication of other ideas in the area from different sources. Together these efforts formed the *cybernetics movement*. However, the term *cybernetics* actually came from another major contributor to this scientific field. Norbert Wiener was a math genius from Missouri who had earlier worked on optimizing automatic anti-aircraft artillery. He was fascinated by the idea of utilizing *feedback* from everyday tools like pumps, air hammers or telephones to gather information. By studying what happens during a mechanical or electronic process, and by automating the collected results of those studies, or the *feedback*, Wiener surmised that he could automate the regulation of the actions performed by the tools he studied. Today we take for granted that our microwave oven functions effectively. But if the microwave oven's rotations and radiation aren't regulated automatically to match the working conditions of the oven, its voltage will fluctuate wildly. So sometimes it might take an hour to make popcorn, other times only three minutes ... or 17 seconds. Wiener postulated that if machines could do what humans do – have an internal conversation about what's happening; then make adjustments based on that awareness, machines could be vastly more efficient. Lots of time, energy and money would be saved. The science associated with such a self-regulating system was dubbed *cybernetics* in Wiener's book: *Cybernetics, or the Control and Communication in the Animal and the Machine*. It was published five years after McCulloch and Pitts's groundbreaking idea of neural networks, and Wiener's book lent a name to what is now a major scientific field which studies how humans and animals function as self-regulatory systems. Hmmm. Systems that can be re-created or simulated by machines...also called robots. Pitts, McCulloch and Wiener have vastly influenced the last 50 years of popular culture. It is because of their ideas that film and literature has been swamped by self-regulating machines with neural networks. At times this is called A.I. – *artificial intelligence.* In 1950 a short story collection by the freakishly prolific Soviet-born American sci-fi writer and polymath Isaac Asimov, *I, Robot,* presented these principles as entertainment, while also discussing the ethical aspects of letting robots into our lives. In 1968, we first heard the eerie, sociopathic calm in the voice of the *HAL 9000,* the supercomputer in Stanley Kubrick's brilliant film *2001 A Space Odyssey.* And in the summer of 1977, *C3PO* introduced himself cybernetically in George Lucas' *Star Wars saying* "And I am *C3PO,* Human-Cyborg Relations." In the 1980s it was William Gibson's *Neuromancer* which expanded the thought of neural networks to an internet-like world. And Arnold Schwarzenegger played a menacing, self-regulating, artificially intelligent killer-cyborg in *The Terminator.* In the 1990s all of humanity was enslaved in a giant, artificially intelligent network called *The Matrix,* and the fascination with A.I. continues to be a part of modern culture. But luckily, the greater part of this scientific research has peaceful purposes, managed by calm and methodical academics, in unspectacular university labs all over the world. Scientists are generally not interested in wrecking the world, but rather in making it a better place.

This positivity is also the driving force for Ala Trusina.

YOU Are A Network

Ala Trusina is a Moldavian scientist and one of the top researchers of cellular networks at the University of California, San Fransisco (UCSF). Just as brain cells function in neural networks, so it is for all the rest of the body's cells – although the types of networks and structures differ. These body structures are precisely what Trusina studies. She also did research in this field at the University of Copenhagen's *Center for Models of Life* with Swedish biologist and physicist Martin Rosvall, whom we'll meet later on in the book. With their colleagues, they are contributing evidence to support the emerging view that the *network* is the essential structure upon which to base scientific thinking – the lens through which we ought to look at the world. Ala Trusina is one of those rare people who are not only charming and attractive, but also possesses an IQ that few in the world can rival. She is also an enthusiastic conversationalist. In fact, when we met for coffee near her office on the UCSF campus, I had to get my intellect in gear and rev up my brain, because Trusina delivers ideas and information with machine gun speed. I couldn't help asking one of the keenest minds in the network field, whether we are seeing networks everywhere now because "networks" and "networking" had become such popular "buzz words." She replied with the fascinating fact that everything in human biology consists of little networks interconnected with larger networks. She likened it to a Russian "babushka" doll of networks that are integral parts of more inclusive networks, each contained within an even larger network. From the microscopic building blocks of our bodies' cells; to the networks our bodies create when they interact; to social networks between people; as she puts it:

"Networks have always been here. We're just discovering them now. When you start this trail of thought, you quickly realize that the world is a big network consisting of smaller networks. Amino acids, the smallest building blocks of proteins are arranged in networks. And then proteins are networked with each other. These protein networks are the building blocks of the cells in the body, which then interact in networks. We already know that brain cells are networked in the brain. But the latest research shows that immunity system cells, T-cells also communicate. The build networks that contain a collective memory of what

they've seen. And then, of course, there are the organs of the body, which in principle is a network, and then you have people interacting in networks. So this goes on at all levels. "

Dr. Trusina switched from the world of physics to biology because she sees biology as the building blocks of physics. Or in her own words:

"Biology is the physics of the 21st century."

Among other things, she is motivated by the fact that this new knowledge of networks can aid in the curing of serious illnesses in the future. By comparing alterations in cellular networks to the way network structures develop in everything from the internet to human social networks, it may be possible to make predictions that aid in disease prevention. Cellular changes are central to the development of Parkinson's, cancer and diabetes. So perhaps this science of networks knowledge holds some answers to the mysteries that have impeded the fighting of these diseases. Type 2 Diabetes Mellitus is what Trusina and her team are working on currently, comparing network structure in the cells to network structure everywhere else. In this case it is a matter of missing or wrong communication between the cells.

Simply put, some cells just don't pick up the phone. Why not?

"In our laboratory, we're studying unfolded protein response right now. When unfolded proteins in cells don't respond properly, it can lead to type 2 diabetes. There's a communication that tells the unfolded protein to stop responding. Next we will be looking at feedback [in that system]."

In summary, Trusina and her colleagues are studying how the two-way communication works in cellular networks, because this may hold the answer to the prevention of Type 2 Diabetes Mellitus. If it becomes possible to engineer a flawless communication between the cells, it will be a great leap forward in the curing of all cellular change-oriented illnesses. In this way Trusina traces a line back to where it all started – McCulloch and Pitts's neural network, and Wiener's self regulatory machine which used feedback for adjustment. Marc Vidal, Ph.D., is another scientist who is making great progress in this field at the moment. At the Dana Farber Cancer Institute at Harvard, Dr. Vidal studies how network science and our knowledge of network behavior may contribute to finding a cure for cancer. He is collaborating with another leading network scientist, Albert-László Barabási (whom we shall return to.) In 2007 they published a study that showed how all major worldwide diseases are interconnected in a mega-network.

How? It's all about genetics.

Scientists across the globe have been tagging and pairing illnesses with specific genes for some time. This means associating certain illnesses with particular genes of the body. Vidal and Barabási have been trying to map how different diseases are related because they have a shared gene malfunction. They discovered that all major diseases can be genetically mapped in a network where they are all connected, with certain centers attracting more relations than others. According to the Vidal-Barabási map, there is a genetic connection between leukemia and obesity – a connection that wasn't obvious earlier. Deafness is genetically tied to heart diseases; and there are only two genetic links between asthma and Parkinson's. By looking at illnesses through this network method, scientists can now discover new aspects to the causes of illness. It is hoped that this, in turn, will lead to finding faster and more effective cures. We have taken a look at the incredibly complex network of networks in our body, and some of the research being done by some of the world's most outstanding scientists. That was the physical side of things, but how about the psychological side? If we look on the purely biological side, Homo Conexus is not significantly different from Industrial Man. But Homo Conexus has an enormously different way of perceiving the world. This perceptual divide may be the biggest difference, the biggest change, and therefore also the most important development in human history since the steam engine.

It's about how Homo Conexus perceives itself.

***

CHAPTER FIVE:

HOMO CONEXUS GETS AN IDENTITY

The youngest segment of the Homo Conexus crowd are often reminded that they are the most selfish, egotistical, narcissistic, unambitious generation ever. Unproductive, self-involved slackers. Well, this makes sense – seen from the perspective of Industrial Man. But these accusations are nothing if not reflections of the inherent difference between Homo Conexus and earlier editions of Homo Sapiens. They are further examples that highlight the fact that Homo Conexus really *does* represent a new way of being human. There are other accusations along the same line: Homo Conexus will never be truly involved in anything because nowadays the flow of information is so fast that they can never commit to anything – because the next something is already on the way! And it doesn't stop there. More slander: Homo Conexus erodes society because Homo Conexus is flighty and disloyal by nature – resulting in widespread divorce; defections from labor unions; willy-nilly abandonment of political or social causes. Homo Conexus is spoiled, refusing to abide by the structures and strictures of previous generations... well, you can add your own.

Young People Nowadays

Industrial Man's opinion of Homo Conexus is reminiscent of the typical way elder generations have always spoken of the young. Here's the main theme: "What's wrong with these brats, anyway?

There was far more respect, better values, more control of things in the old days."

It seems to have always been thus. Even Socrates (469 B.C – 399 B.C.), who, by the way, is not known to have ever *written* anything, is quoted as saying:

"Today's children love luxury. They have bad manners, contempt for authority; they show disrespect for elders and love chatter in place of exercise. Children are now tyrants, not the servants of their households. They no longer rise when elders enter the room. They contradict their parents, chatter before company, gobble up dainties at the

Since the notion of "The Teenager" was invented in the 1950s, this Socrates quote has often been used to underscore the fact that the rebellious nature of teens has been present throughout history.

The only problem: there's no convincing evidence that Socrates ever said this.

There are many verifiable Socrates quotes, some dealing with youth issues (for instance, in Plato's *The State)*. But none probes the depths that the above quote does. The internet is bubbling with discussions about where that quote may have originated. One possible source is *Personality and Adjustment* (1953) by William L. Patty and Louise S. Johnson. This psychology book was written just as youth began defining itself as a "culture" in the 1950s. Another source is said to be Gijsbert van Hall, mayor of Amsterdam from 1957 to 1967, who, in an article printed in *The New York Times* on April 3rd, 1966, reacted to a demonstration with the same quote, which he also attributed to Socrates. (You can find the article on the newspaper's website by searching for his name and the date at *www.nyt.com*.) Later on the quote was included in an editorial by Malcolm S. Forbes (1919-1990), the founder of the financial magazine that carries his surname. His researchers tried – as did many after them – to find the quote among Socrates' statements, but to no avail. They ended up calling Gijsbert van Hall to ask where *he* had gotten the quote. He didn't remember, but he believed he had read it in a Dutch book once. The Socrates quote seems to be more like something people need to hear, than a certified historical fact. Almost like an "urban legend" from ancient times, that takes on a life of its own. A pre-internet viral campaign. The Greek thinker and poet Hesiod, who lived about 300 years before Socrates, is alleged to have said something similar, but this is equally hard to confirm. But it's the content, not the author, that matters here. Give some thought to what went on inside of you when you read that quote. Did it make you feel at ease? To feel like laughing at how parental generations have always thought their children were spoiled – how everything was "better in the old days"? Or did it make you curious? Did you feel like Googling the quote to see what else Socrates had said, or find out where the quote came from? If the first instance is the case, then your acceptance of traditional authority is probably intact. The reasoning: well, if it says so in a relatively serious, well laid-out book like this one, it's most likely true. This is a classic feature of Industrial Man. But if you were curious – if the quote sparked your critical sense when it comes to what the media serves up – then you probably have much more in common with Homo Conexus. The difference is that Homo Conexus, through his entire upbringing, has had access to a wide variety of sources of information, who all thought they alone had the truth. How do you assess which one is the most reliable? You don't. To Homo Conexus all media platforms are equal. Whether something is true or false is up to the individual, and not authorized by a specific medium. This kind of social constructivism, based on equally important media input, is typical to Homo Conexus – but *not* to Industrial Man, who typically prefers certain media to others. The baby-boomer cohort – those born just after World War II – would often rather believe news that comes from the radio or the newspaper than from TV. Their children find the news on TV more credible than their parents do. Homo Conexus doesn't think one medium is any more credible than another. But just as the network generation isn't ripe with technical wizards just because they grew up in a time with an abundance of technology, Homo Conexus isn't better at source criticism just because they consider all media equally credible. It is still a highly personal issue whether one is suspicious of media input or not. The difference is that a book, like the one in your hand right now, is not necessarily any more credible to Homo Conexus because it is a book – whereas Industrial Man, who grew up with books as his primary source of knowledge in school, in college and at work, has a tendency to think that it is. How can you as a reader be sure that the Socrates story is valid? Well, you really can't – and I'd rather not let on that I hold the definitive truth. But the story of the Socrates quote shows us two things that have changed with the transition to the network society, things that affect Homo Conexus's way of being human. Maybe you already know of Socrates's 2,300-year-old skeptical portrait of youth, using arguments that resemble the ones you heard from your own parents. Maybe you heard the quote from friends, or read about it somewhere. Quotes that resonate with the public generally survive the test of time, even when they aren't founded on truth. As I mentioned, that quote was dismissed as attributable to Socrates as early as the 1960s. But even so, we still talk about it today, 40 years later. The quote hasn't lost its appeal even though it has been "debunked." That's partly because it's a *useful* quote, but also because it wasn't easy for everybody to see its "unveiling" until recently. Until the breakthrough of the internet it was an exceptionally time consuming matter to research such a subject. You'd have to go to the library and sift through Plato's writings about Socrates to look for the quote. And, sitting among the stacks of some high-ceilinged, genteel old library in San Francisco, Buenos Aires or Copenhagen, how would you have found the connection to the mayor of Amsterdam mentioned in *The New York Times* in 1966? And would Patty and Johnson's book, not to mention Malcolm Forbes's editorial, have been likely to pop up in your research? It would take days, even weeks, to have tracked those items down.

But thanks to internet search engines, it took me around 10 minutes to find the information I have passed on here – including fact confirmation from three different sources. I even found a searchable online version of Plato's *The State*. Then it was only a question of cross-searching for "youth" in order to find out whether the quote was actually a part of the antique scripture.

Now we know it wasn't.

Another issue which has changed with the coming of the network society, and which affects Homo Conexus's way of being, is the greatly enhanced ability to draw on other people's experiences. It's one thing that it was possible to find information about Socrates' quote – or lack of it – relatively fast, because search engines are our primary gateways to information on the internet today. It's another matter that a lot of the information we do find is *the result of other people's info searches*. Example: I didn't find out that Malcolm Forbes's team of researchers had called the mayor of Amsterdam, Gijsbert van Hall, to learn where he found Socrates's quote. That research was relayed by a guy in a discussion forum about quotes, which turned up when I Googled the quote. And if you go to this web address:

http://www.qis.net/~jschmitz/afu/youth.htm

…you can even read an exchange of information between scholars and public librarians about this particular quote. It reveals, among other things, that Forbes used the quote, but that his researchers couldn't find the source. One librarian went through the magazine database – physical, paper magazines, that is – to find this fact, then replied to an e-mail, which came up again in an online discussion forum in August of 2000.

Because this information, this dialogue and these experiences are flowing freely on the internet, they are all accessible by search engines. This shows how fast the spread of knowledge has accelerated since the popular breakthrough of the internet in the mid-1990s. It's also an example of how reality's complexity can no longer be hidden. While Industrial Man could make do with only a few sources of information, Homo Conexus insists on being informed from as many sources as possible – preferably all the time. The world is complex; it always was. But it used to be simplified for us by the limited number of media we used. If you were a blue collar worker in the 1950s, you got virtually all your information from working class media, probably morning or evening daily newspapers, supplemented by the news on the radio. Clearly more rarified information was available to the upper classes via higher-toned media (specialty magazines; learnèd periodicals; documentaries; even lecture series and seminars). But in general, Industrial Man consumed media that corresponded with the values and the identity of the working man, and which served to preserve those values and that identity. Industrial Man's choice of media both fit and shaped the identity of Industrial Man. It isn't like that anymore. Due to the dizzyingly rapid spread of knowledge, and the consequent equalization of the authority of different media, the information landscape is now a complex mass of info-bombardment. And *this* is the world Homo Conexus has grown up in, and has learned to navigate from the very beginning. The ability to absorb and process huge quantities of information quickly, sifting through a vast array of sources, is one of the abilities Homo Conexus has – but which Industrial Man *doesn't* have.

It's Only About People

And it's not only about the media. It's just as much about interpersonal communication. As mentioned in Chapter Three, Leonard Kleinrock told me that he didn't realize what he had created, until his 97-year old mother sent him an e-mail. Bob Taylor saw it coming and put it down in writing. To both of them, the nerdy IT math experiment that was the creation of the internet in the 1960s and 1970s, morphed into a social phenomenon. That everyone on the planet could now share knowledge, and communicate faster than ever, was the true jackpot in the creation of the internet. Looking back, Taylor and Kleinrock don't consider the technology, but rather the consequent binding together of people, their gift to the world. To recall the Socrates quote once again, the salient point isn't just the fact that *I* can find information quickly, or that *I'm* being bombarded with a constant stream of information. It's also about my constantly bombarding *others* with information – *I contribute information to the flow*. The lickety-split two-way communication is as much a part of the change that defines the identity of Homo Conexus as the info bombardment itself is. If individual citizens hadn't contributed to the information flow in my search for the source of the false Socrates quote, it would have been much harder to find both the *New York Times* and the Malcolm Forbes editorial. Indeed, if others hadn't mentioned them in the internet forum to which we all now have access, it's unlikely I would ever have stumbled upon them. It would have had to be purely by chance. And depending upon chance is not a reliable research strategy. The massive flow of information in the world today consists of both concrete facts and also little information fragments. And because they can both be created and conveyed so quickly, it has become necessary for Homo Conexus to develop a more advanced ability to find, process and absorb information, than Industrial Man ever had. Information flows in and out of Homo Conexus, as intuitively as air flowing in and out of his lungs, whereas Industrial Man turns the collection and distribution of information on and off with his consciousness. That the networked man participates naturally and instinctively in dialogues on the network, and that Industrial Man doesn't is a difference of vast importance. I will dare to say that this difference also means a great deal to the way the old type of human, and the new, perceives himself and the surrounding world. And that the time has come to break away from the way we humans have perceived ourselves for the past 400-500 years.

Goodnight, René

When René Descartes published his *Meditations On First Philosophy* in 1641, he postulated a consciousness of the separation between subject and object. That an individual can be considered a self-conscious, thinking being, who through his senses perceives the world as a collection of objects. Since then this separation has been part of the way we view ourselves. We perceive the world, and from this perception we create an image of ourselves. At some point in our childhood we cease to live solely instinctively. The auto-pilot goes off. We start wondering who we are; why we are; where we are; how we sense things – and how we appear to others. We cease to just live happy-go-luckily, and start considering our actions before acting. In our teens we begin wearing special clothes, listening to certain types of music, and hanging out with certain kinds of people – because there are values in those clothes, that music and those people that we would like to identify with. Or put another way, we would like to inhabit the identity that goes with those values. We create our own self-image, our identity. And even though this changes throughout our lives, it is still shaped by the way we interpret the input presented to us through our senses. We perceive the objects – as Descartes has it – and process them within us. We absorb some things. We throw others away. We ponder the information harvested by our senses, and create new thoughts about it. This process produces a set of values, feelings and thoughts which we choose to make our own. And this is how we become a subject – an individual with an identity consisting of a collection of processed inputs. A collection which is frequently updated at the rate that we experience new things, and add more information through our senses. This is the founding idea of Western philosophy, a cornerstone of our society. We wouldn't even be speaking about differing views on different subjects, and the right to think freely and alternatively, if Descartes hadn't established that we, as humans, can reflect upon the information relayed to us by our senses. It's a fundamental principle of Western democracy that different perceptions of reality must be allowed to co-exist, because we all have different ways of perceiving sensory input. Because we, as individuals, create our identities from input received in the course of different phases of our lives, we are potentially all a little different from one another. The right to be different is the foundation of freedom of speech. So we see the importance of Descartes to the way Western man has been shaped, and how he has organized himself in societies.

That is, until now.

There happens to be a great difference between the world today, and the world that existed before the evolution of the Network Society. The input available, from which we created our identities, used to come at a pace we could keep up with. But today the pace is much quicker. This acceleration of the amount of input we must constantly process has had dramatic impact. Whereas we only used to get input from our own cultural sphere, now our input includes the whole world's cornucopia of cultures and philosophies, crowding into our awareness second by second. There have never been so many opinions and facts to choose among as there are today. By growing up in this new lightning-fast version of the world, Homo Conexus has become fundamentally different from Industrial Man.

More Than You'd Want to Read

Here's one example of how much information is currently pumped into our society, as opposed to earlier times. The *How Much Information* project is an ongoing initiative, begun in 2000 at UC Berkeley in California. The object: to measure how much information is being produced and distributed in the Network Society. This originally resulted in two reports from Berkeley, in 2001 and 2003, before the project went into hiatus. It is now run by the UC San Diego, who updated the statistics in 2009. The program delivers a clear image of the unimaginably gigantic universe of information being produced and circulated in today's Network Society. In 2009, researchers calculated that the amount of information produced and consumed in 2008 in the U.S. alone totaled 3.6 *zettabytes.* This may not sound impressive until you stop to realize how much a zettabyte really is. It's one million times one million gigabyte. The world's largest library is the Library of Congress in Washington, D.C. The Library has the equivalent of 528 miles of shelves that hold books and other publications. To shelve the 3.6 zettabytes of information just mentioned – the info just from the year 2008 – we would need 14.4 million libraries the size of the Library of Congress.

Please take a moment to digest that idea. It's not peanuts.

Now consider this: When Berkeley did their last survey in 2002, a mere seven years before UC San Diego took over, they measured the consumption of information to be "just" 23 exabytes - or 89,900 Libraries of Congress. That's a staggering growth. The 2009 numbers equals more than 760,000,000 miles of bookshelves. You could build bookshelves that stretch from Planet Earth to the Moon more than 3,100 times just to store that information! UC San Diego claims 3.6 zettabytes is 34 gigabytes of information per American per day. Now, you may think you know how much 34 gigabytes is from looking at the hard drive or the files on your laptop or your mp3 player. But it only gets truly staggering when you think of it in terms of books. One letter or character in a book equals one byte of information. The average book contains roughly 600,000 characters. Divide 34 billion bytes by 600,000, and you get 56,666.67. In other words: even if you only had to consume your little share of the new information pumped into the Network Society every year, you would have to read more than 56,000 books a day.

56,000 books a day!

You'll probably agree that's a fair amount of data; a great deal of input we'd need to sort through, every single day. And that's only the United States. Then think about the same production of information going on in Europe, China, Australia, India, Japan... Time for another image. Picture that the your identity is formed by painting yourself in different colors which represent your values, thoughts and perceptions. In the Industrial Society, you'd walk casually among the tins of paint, look them over, dip the brush in your colors of choice, and start painting yourself. But in the Network Society, other people are swarming around you with paint guns, firing new colors at you every half a second. You're getting splattered in a cross-fire of colors, including some new shades you have never seen before. That palette corresponds to the sum total of impressions on the pages of those four new books you'd read every day. Metaphorically speaking, for Homo Conexus, identity formation boils down to leaping in front of the gun, taking the splashes and occasionally ducking if they see a color coming in that they don't like. This illustrates the difference between the way Homo Conexus forms his identity, and the way Industrial Man did and still does to an extent. Identity forms and develops much more quickly for Conexus. There are many more shades on the color palette, combining to form one's total identity. But most crucially, there is a significant difference when it comes to the prioritizing of colors. The Industrial Man will typically spend much time finding and using his "favorite color" first. But in the Network Society there is far less time to think about the swirling blizzard of incoming colors. Leaving our rather strained paint analogy, it means that Homo Conexus, to a greater extent than the Industrial Man, gives equal status to the many inputs shaping his identity. To those with values and identity rooted in the Industrial Man background, job and family are the overwhelmingly important inputs. I maintain that Homo Conexus differs on this point. Just as Homo Conexus doesn't have any favorite media that hold a monopoly on truth, there aren't any *other* sources of information that hold the ultimate truth. Parents today complain more than earlier generations about having trouble "reaching" and "understanding" their children. Teachers at all levels find it a greater challenge to keep young people's attention than used to be the case. And correspondingly, respect for teachers has declined noticeably. On the everyday level, it is harder e.g. for youth counselors to persuade young people to turn up, when they have already registered for an activity. Time, place and appointments don't represent the same value as before – because new, exciting possibilities turn up at a faster rate than ever. This makes the perceived value of any one individual possibility decrease.What is happening here is really a decentralization.Decentralization is an inherent feature of the changes that take place in the transition from the Industrial Society to the Network Society. More on that in Chapter Seven.

Pity The Poor Social Workers

Thanks to a book I wrote with Julie Ralund called *Generation Network* I have been lucky enough to give a number of talks to gatherings of teachers and youth counselors. It is always with a certain amount of awe and respect that I appear in front of these assemblies. I may have studied the topic, and talked to many young people, but these counselors are the heroes who deal with kids every day. From their experience, they not only know about, but *feel* the gap between Industrial and Connected Humans. They should know much more than I about these youths – and they do. All I can do is to help them see their own experiences from a new angle, which helps them bridge the divide between Industrial and Connected Humans. Youth club counselors, if anyone, are victims of decentralization. The youth club staff used to be a "central" resource, to whom young people could go to have activities suggested to them, or simply to get personal advice. Now this authority has been largely taken from counselors. Some have told me about field trips or other activities that require prior registration – but which get only a 20% turnout on the appointed day. It used to be 20% that *didn't* show up – now it's the other way around! As those who have been in the job long enough can testify, this tendency has been creeping in over the course of the past seven to ten years – which coincides interestingly with the time span that produced the latest generation of Network children. When they ask me why this is, I point to decentralization. Youth counselors are no longer central to young people's activities. The kids can do their own thing, thank you very much. It has always been young peoples' wish to do their own thing – it's part of growing up. But this generation doesn't even need teachers' or counselors' acceptance – let alone their help or knowledge – to get started. They just get things going. This is largely due to the fact that *many activities today are based on the digital domain*. But even if the young people's activities in a youth club aren't specifically digital, like console games or computer games, net surfing or communicating via cell phones, then they can at least be organized digitally. For example, like booking soccer practice by computer, or registering for some activity via text messages or on the club's website. That way, counselors become an equal player in the youths' network. Youth clubs used to be centralized networks, the center being the facility and the faculty. But to Homo Conexus these are now just other parts of the overall paradigm of spare time. Just other possibilities among the millions of possibilities available all the time. And they keep coming. When I tell them about all this, youth counselors usually get that weary look. I comfort them by saying that even Network People need hubs – (see Chapter Seven) – centers in their lives, to which they can return in order to get elsewhere on their journeys. I usually tell them that they should appreciate their new role as "equal players" in young people's networks, because now they no longer need to try so hard to "get down" with the kids. If they just make their experience visibly available to them, the kids will come to them when they feel the need to benefit from the counselors' experiences. And this is usually more often than one would think. The way a hub works is that it's not so much "a place where you hang," as it is *a place you return to* in order to set off on new adventures. Parallel: an airport is very rarely anyone's final destination. Whether you fly, drive or walk there, you almost always go to an airport to go somewhere else

– a conference or other business at or near the airport, or even more likely onto another plane bound for a third destination. In the same way my advice to youth counselors is not to work so hard to make their young people dependent on the club. But rather work to make it a hub they will always go back to (until they're too old) to find new inspiration – and create new networks.

A New Identity

As we have seen, where there was once a centralized interpersonal organization between kids and teachers or counselors, now a more evenly distributed, decentralized structure exists. This structure doesn't come from outside, but from *within* the Homo Conexus identity. I believe that Homo Conexus perceives the world as decentralized, unlike the Industrial Man who looks at the world as centralized, with himself at the center. This is the model of the identity image that the Western World has used since the Renaissance: the individual is at the center, like a subject observing the surrounding world. This individual forms his/her identity from sensory input, and creates values, thoughts and attitudes from that input. Closest to the individual are the so-called "close-to-home" things: family, friends, job, cultural background – all things that shape the individual emotionally and empirically throughout life. This centralistic model does not encourage a great deal of change. Change is more likely to happen in other modalities.

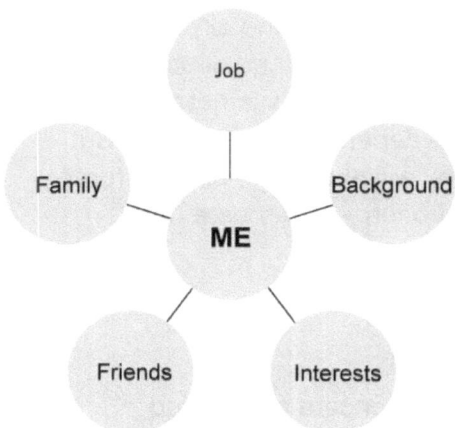

Industrial Man's Centralistic Identity

If you are the type who builds identity by being in opposition to other groups of society (e.g., Proud Worker vs. Rich Employer; Environmentalist vs. Heavy Consumer; Health Freak vs. Hedonist, etc.), then changes will usually take place in the group you belong to, long before the change takes place in you. If there's a change, say, in the workplace, it has an effect on the underlying structure. It will almost certainly impact the individual at the center. Or, in other words, if you get a new colleague or a new desk or a new assignment within your position, it has a great impact on you. This is because, as shown in the illustration, the "job" circle is placed very near the core, only one link away from the self. And that's how it always is for Industrial Man in regards to the role his plays in creating his identity. Industrial Man's life is defined by his livelihood, and that's "Job" is only one link away.

You would still state, if someone should ask more than your name, that you're a carpenter, salesman or journalist. You would be unlikely to identify yourself as a philatelist, soccer fan or karaoke singer – even though one of those may bring far greater pleasure to you, enhancing your quality of life.

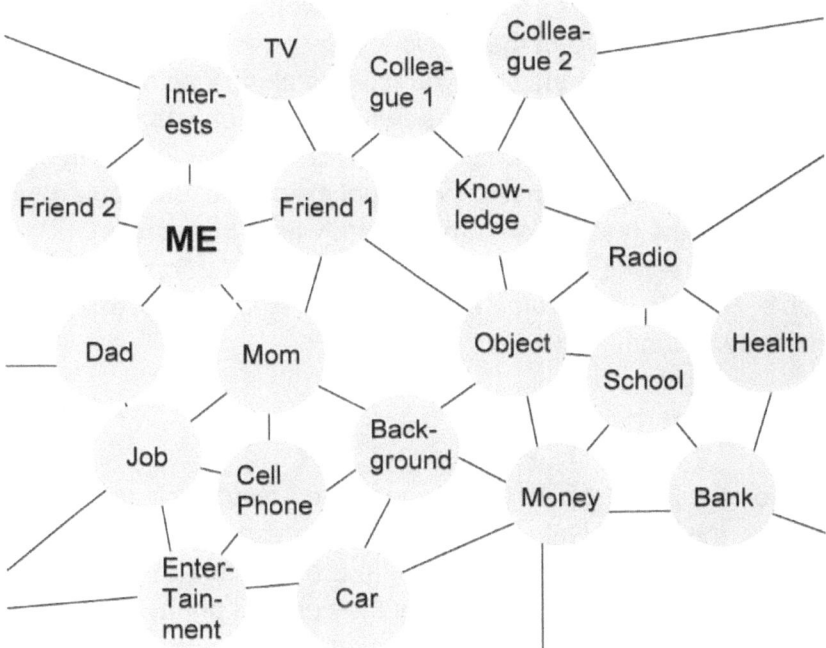

Identity Formation In Homo Conexus. Note that the network has no limitations, but continues beyond the frame of the illustration. Also note that the lines (or links) around the immediate network surrounding "ME" are heavier than the other links, to illustrate the difference between strong and weak links in the network.

To Homo Conexus, life is a continuous stream of endless possibilities that keep popping up in the shape of new network connections. Every time a new person is added to the network, a new opening to another network – and another and another ad infinitum – presents itself, leading to geometrically more new possibilities. Every time a new activity or a new object becomes part of the personal network of Homo Conexus, it comes with new features that pave the way in turn for new networks and possibilities. And because of the dazzling speed with which Homo Conexus receives new input, changes in the network are fast, and new sections are constructed frequently. You are not the undisputed center of your own universe, nor do you perceive yourself in opposition to others in the network, but you rather see yourself as a creature of the network you are in. When the network changes around you, you change along with it; form connections to other points in the network; and constantly find new hubs leading to new challenges. This may sound like an erosion of the self-dependent individual, even a kind of forced collectivism like fascism or communism, where individuals subject themselves to the *Greater Good* of *The Nation* or *The People*. But this is far from being the case – indeed it's really the other way around.

Neo-Solidarity

In the beginning of this chapter I mentioned how Generation Network, the Digital Natives, were often accused of being narcissistic and egotistical. It's easy to arrive at this misconception if we look at the way they upload phony glamour pictures of themselves to social websites, and describe themselves in bloated self-satisfied profiles and blogs. Pair this image with their thoroughly critical approach to new products, new input, new phenomena and new information, and it's easy to believe that what we have is a spoiled rotten, self-centered generation.

I'm sorry, but I have to claim that they aren't like that.

First let me state that the notion of solidarity is on the verge of a solid comeback – albeit in a slightly more cynical way. I'll deal more thoroughly with that subject in the chapter on Homo Conexus and the workplace. But for now let me introduce this neo-solidarity as "cynical solidarity" or "merchant's solidarity." What do I mean by that? Just this. The traditional view of solidarity is based on two pillars. One: it's a good thing to help others, because one day you may be the one needing help. The other: a whole group of people has more weight than the voice of an individual. But as many trade unions realize these days, not many people buy into these ideas. It's a fact that it is harder than ever for unions to attract young members, let alone make young people understand why joining a union is a good thing in the first place! Was Homo Conexus born conservative? No, it's just that – once again – it's due to the drive for decentralization. The networks of the Network Society are primarily decentralized, as we will see in Chapter Seven. When trying to maintain a centralistic, hierarchical organization in a society leaning more and more towards decentralization, it's like trying to fit a brick (or an old cell phone) into a round hole. Decentralization is such a strong part of the Network Society's spirit that Homo Conexus has adopted the decentralized structure as a way of structuring identity. At the point where one's perception of self is a living, breathing decentralized structure, it's hard to fit that self into a centralized structure. The old idea of "solidarity" is also centralistic. Of course, it wasn't to begin with, when workers from various trades first started organizing in guilds. The guilds were small scale and specialized before they were amalgamated into the gigantic unions we know today. Originally, guilds and unions were small networks where you would care for your own kind first. The welders wouldn't care too much about other iron workers, weavers weren't particularly interested in the needs of other textile workers. And that was a decentralized, if hardly altruistic, idea. Later on, as unions and guilds merged, you would have to consider everyone in the group. Unions became one massive unit, which could be strong and raise a more powerful voice in negotiations. The idea of solidarity went from being something you showed towards those closest to you, to being something that was imposed on you from above in the organization. Thereby the idea of solidarity became centralistic – especially because it was often some centrally placed people who asked you to join in. In the case of Homo Conexus, neo-solidarity is decentralized and optional. You can opt out, but once you are part of the network, you have to show solidarity due to the nature of the network itself. You have to engage in reciprocal actions with your other networkers to stay "online". If you don't engage, this basically means resigning from society. In Chapter Four, I mentioned the many similarities between computer networks and human networks. Similarities that have natural explanations since computer networks were originally based on the structure of the neural networks of our brains. But in order to explain the principle of solidarity in Homo Conexus, we need to look at the computers again. When two computers are hooked up via a computer network they constantly confirm that they're connected to each other – that they are both on line on the same network. This is called "pinging." It's a maritime expression where the use of sonars and echo sounders are used to measure the distance of objects underneath the surface of the water. This is done by sending a sound (a "ping") through the water, and timing how long it takes before the echo comes back. The information is then transcribed into meters, yards or feet. Likewise a computer can "ping" another computer on the same network – not with sound, but with a data string which is to be returned to the transmitting computer. If the transmitting computer receives the returned data from the receiving computer within a certain time, it concludes that both computers are still in touch and that the flow of data is functional. As we will see in Chapter Eight, this is precisely the same mechanism that is at work when two teenagers are sending each other mindless text messages, such as "Hi" to which the other replies "Wuzzup?" It's not the message's meaning that is important. What matter to them is *the confirmation that they are still online with each other.* The "merchant's solidarity" works in the same way in Homo Conexus. In order to stay a part of the network that creates identity in Homo Conexus, he or she must take an active part in the network. It won't work to just stay passive, because then you lose the attraction that makes others want to link to you. You lose network connections and possibilities for action. So it's a matter of making sure that the points in the network can see you, and that they stay interested. This is done by making oneself known in a number of ways. To teenagers it may be done by uploading pictures of oneself to the net, or going on at length about oneself on a social network profile page. To the older part of the Homo Conexus crowd it may mean sending instant messages or text messages just to keep the line vibrant. But the most effective of maintaining the connection is through the exchange of social currency (as we will see in chapters Eight and Nine), like links to entertaining videos, text messaged jokes or even music files that are shared in the name of keeping each other's "networkship." It's somewhat merchant-like: "If I do this for you, then I can count on you doing something for me – because we don't want to lose the possibilities that come from the fact that we are linked." So this solidarity isn't ideological, but pragmatic. And it has already proven much more efficient than traditional solidarity, as we will see in the following chapters – also when it comes to issues that the unions are fighting for.

Social Currency

This new way of looking at solidarity is a kind of evolution of the solidarity definitions advanced by social philosopher Émile Durkheim. In his principal work, 1893's *De La Division Du Travail Social*, he distinguishes between mechanical and organic solidarity. The first is a type of given solidarity of the kind that isn't rational, for instance religious solidarity forced by dogma. The organic solidarity on the other hand is rational, and leaves much more room for the individual. According to Durkheim it is the specialized skills of the individuals that make them dependent upon each other. It is that which the individuals, because of their special skills, can do for each other which creates solidarity. A carpenter and a mason should have solidarity for one and other, because their individual skills are needed to build a house, and the solidarity should also include the person who made the tools, and the person who drew the blueprint for the house. They all play their part in the social structure that comes into play when a house is being built. According to Durkheim, solidarity comes into existence because the task couldn't be carried out without the participation of all of those involved. The carpenter needs the mason who needs the toolmaker, etc., to get the job done. Durkheim's definition is the classic multidisciplinary idea of solidarity, which the working class movement has clung to for a century. The solidarity of the Network Society, however, expands Durkheim's idea of solidarity. Now not only professional skills, but also social and interpersonal skills – and networking opportunities – are elements and qualities the participant needs. In other words: the solidarity that binds Homo Conexus "natives" together is a matter of how others in the network can help you expand your network, and what you can add on the social end. It's not only about how you function in work-related circumstances. This is part and parcel of the blurring of the line between private life and work, which is also a part of Homo Conexus.

I Link, Therefore I Am

So one explanation of the decentralized structure of Network Man's identity is that the most fertile possibilities come from being a strong point in a greater network. By becoming a person that others wish to connect to, one can derive maximum benefit from the equalized structure of the network. Therefore the identity of Homo Conexus is based upon the inclusion of others in its formation, and that his identity evolves more rapidly than that of Industrial Man. Descartes, mentioned earlier in this chapter, was also the man behind the immortal philosophical words Cogito, ergo sum, which is usually translated as I think, therefore I am. What Descartes meant was, that the only proof man had that the world around him existed was the fact that "something" was having that very thought. Even if that "something" could think that the world around it might possibly be an illusion, then that "something" would have to *be*.

But for Homo Conexus, we need to rephrase a little: I link, therefore I am.

Homo Conexus is nothing without the network. Homo Conexus only exists because of the connection with others. This is why it's more important to Homo Conexus to constantly make sure that the entire network is OK, not just local parts of it. The network is more important than the job, because if you lose your job, you can find another one through your network. The network is more important than family, because if you lose a family member the network will help you get through the process of the mourning, or even the practical circumstances in relation to a funeral.

Social Currency - not Social Capital

This is also the reason why sharing has become such a vital part of the network society. You share music by sending files to each other. You send funny videos and comments to one another using Instant Messaging clients. You share your mood with the friends on the social networks by writing your status on Facebook or tweeting on Twitter. You share your current location on Foursquare. Google Latitude and Facebook Places. All of this is not a simple question of disproportionate openness. It's because sharing is one of the easiest ways to keep the line vibrant to all points in your network. What you share over your network has been dubbed "social currency" by the American media philosopher Douglas Rushkoff, about whom you will read more later. Social currency is something you exchange, whereas "social capital" is something you save and accumulate. This is how Rushkoff defines social currency:

"Social currency is like a good joke. When a bunch of friends sit around and tell jokes, what are they really doing? Entertaining one another? Sure, for a start. But they are also using content — mostly unoriginal content that they've heard elsewhere — in order to lubricate a social occasion. And what are most of us doing when we listen to a joke? Trying to memorize it so that we can bring it somewhere else."

Think about this the next time you curse the lousy jokes that are jamming your Inbox. The senders believe they're sending you a present, but it's really just an excuse to interact with you. If the joke is good enough, the social currency is worth enough for you to give the sender a reply. Whatever else Homo Conexus shares to keep the connection to the other points in the network flowing is social currency. And the exchanging of this is almost as important to the social cohesion in Homo Conexus's world, as real currency is to the financial markets. However, to define oneself through the connection with others does mean a great deal to the practical situations Homo Conexus engages in. Homo Conexus makes new demands of the workplace; new demands of the selection at the supermarket; new demands for media content; and new demands when it comes to the usefulness of products and services he purchases. These new value sets are the subject of the following chapters. Let's start right where most of us spend the lion's share of our waking hours: in the workplace. Homo Conexus is entering that workplace in droves, and even though it's not raining jobs right now, Homo Conexus demands such fundamental change from his employers, that it's making many a manager's hair turn grey prematurely.

***

CHAPTER SIX:

HOMO CONEXUS GOES TO WORK

During the writing of this book, 20-year old Joey started in a trainee-position in a medium-sized IT-company. The 52-year-old receptionist thought Joey was cute. He still had a youthful enthusiastic aura, long gone from most other people she smiled at every morning. Joey seldom replied to her smile with anything more than a semi-grumpy "'morning." Yet like all good receptionists, she knew all about what was going on in the company, including with Joey. So she knew that Joey was getting on Kevin, his department manager's, nerves. It was unproductive to send him memos about meetings, because he didn't always get around to picking up meeting notices sent via Outlook. And when Joey did show up for a meeting, it was with his cell phone on "silent" – but not turned off. It would lie on the table, and if a text message arrived he would reply to it instantly. But what got on the department manager's nerves the most, was that Joey didn't even seem to lose his concentration when that happened. *How did he pull it off?* When Kevin came out with a cup of coffee in his hands, and spilled his guts to the motherly receptionist, he told her how he was just getting used to people bringing laptops to meetings, and they were on. But now he'd have to get used to there being both cell phones *and* laptops – and that text messages and instant messages were always answered immediately, even during the meeting. But conversely, it would take ages to get a reply when Kevin sent an e-mail to Joey.

It was as if it was a result of him doing all these things simultaneously that Joey's efficiency level was higher than his colleagues'. He performed well, when you looked at the net results. Kevin would also tell the receptionist how Joey had solved problems that others in the company had toiled at for a year. When asked about it, Joey would say that he had consulted friends, and friends of friends in his network, but in a way that didn't jeopardize the safety of the company. But what surprised the receptionist the most was when Kevin had told her about Joey's job interview. When Kevin together with the head of Human Resources, and the employee representative had asked the young pup the mandatory question "Where would you like to be, career-wise, five years down the line?" he had simply replied: "Not here." (Blasphemy! Sacrilege!) That layabout even took the liberty of expressing excitement with the fact that the job was *limited* to two years, with the possibility of an extension. But this surprising attitude came across in such a kind, sincere and refreshing way, that it was impossible to perceive it as impertinence. And it didn't seem like the job was unimportant to Joey. In fact, he seemed inclined to give it his very best shot, while he was holding the position. But he had made it clear from the beginning that he would move on eventually, preferably within the measurable near future. It was much easier to talk about the salary. That part was over and done with very quickly...

New Job = New Network = New Possibilities

Kevin, Joey's department manager, told me this story, and the names have been changed for obvious reasons. It happened in a company which, like so many others, is trying to adjust to the work habits of Homo Conexus. For that very reason the company prefers to remain anonymous. But this story could have been told by virtually any modern company. I keep hearing these kinds of anecdotes all around, especially when I lecture to big labor union leaderships or boards of directors at large corporations.

Like the fact that young Homo Conexus natives like jobs with limited time lines. One union representative told me that her company had hired many young people in their early 20s, but within the past couple of years, she'd seen a new tendency: Today's young people preferred temporary positions, and didn't try to hide their plans for moving on in the future. Yet she didn't have the impression that they were just looking for a place where they could make the most money. So, when I explained that Homo Conexuses were constantly pursuing new opportunities for expanding their network, it finally made sense to her. The position her company was offering wasn't something that the Homo Conexus just wanted "over and done with" in order to get a monthly salary – but rather an important step in the newly employed person's progress. To Homo Conexus, it is important that the place they spend most of their day, should also be the best possible investment in *new possibilities. It's a matter of the job presenting new points in the network – new hubs from which they can move on.* Since the incident mentioned above, I have given many talks to other people in hiring positions from HR conferences to leadership seminars. I always ask whether they have had the same experience. They usually have. They see, to an ever-greater extent, young people admitting that for them, the workplace is part of an ongoing progress – not just a nice place to make a living. And there's a natural limit on how long they stay with any one company. It seems to parallel the limit on how much one can expand a network within a company, with a limited amount of employees, all working on the same limited products, or within the same area.

The Top 8 Job Features

Earlier generations found job security, career opportunities and friendships by staying with the same company for many years. Colleague relationships often morphed from the purely professional into the private sphere. And if you stayed with your company long enough there was a good chance you could *climb the ladder*, as far as promotions went. The longer you were there, the deeper your roots were, and the harder it was to fire you. But all those workplace values belong to *Industrial Society*. The very ideas of "up" and "down" – or even "ladder" – are meaningless in the Network Society. As I will cover in the following pages, Homo Conexus doesn't think "up" or "down" – but rather *outwards*. This first came to my attention when, a couple of years ago, I was asked to moderate a panel on why young people no longer found it attractive to work in the IT industry. Before the panel began, I was handed a list of job features. It was the results of a survey of a group of young people who were asked to prioritize the features that were most important to them when choosing a job. The list looked like this:

1. *I can grow and find new challenges.*

2. *There is a spirit of solidarity among the colleagues.*

3. *I can do something for others.*

4. *The salary is good.*

5. *The work isn't too stressful.*

6. *There is little chance of being fired.*

7. *I have plenty of time off.*

8. *The job is prestigious.*

This list made me very happy – it confirmed a hunch I had. This *Top 8* says a great deal about how Homo Conexus will contribute to the workplaces of the future, and it confirms that the network is valued above all else for Homo Conexus. The three most important features about the future jobs of these youths, *are all network oriented.*

The undisputed winner is *"That I can grow and find new challenges."* This is exactly what's making the abovementioned youngster's ticker tock. And it's what Human Resources personnel experience first hand, when young Homo Conexuses come in for job interviews. A job is an opportunity for growth, not just a place to make some money. It's another step on a journey where both the destination and the duration of the endeavor is completely unknown. The worst thing that can happen to Homo Conexus professionally is stagnation. And this is a logical fact. His whole life, Homo Conexus has been bombarded with impressions from all around, and has forged his identity from this world view, as seen in the last chapter. There would be an imbalance felt in a Network Person's life, if eight waking hours were spent in stagnation, while the rest of the day was pure network flow. Homo Conexus people feel compelled to choose jobs that match the journey they are on in other parts of their lives. This makes self-development important, just like "new challenges" – the other half of entry #1 among the top 8. What will an industrial person write to his colleagues when changing jobs? "I'm seeking new challenges, and therefore I'm leaving my position... blah, blah." Homo Conexus demands that these new challenges come *without* the job-change – that *the job itself* constantly create new challenges. But the two most important surprises on the list to me are #4 and #8. The fact that compensation takes fourth place after more social criteria was quite surprising to me, as was the notion that Homo Conexus apparently won't take a job just because *others* find it prestigious. That was definitely not the case when I grew up as a generation X'er, when the yuppie movement reveled in extravagant salaries, and having the right logo on your gold-embossed business card was everything! Homo Conexus's take on money and prestige will be dealt with in greater length later on in this chapter. First, let's put things into a little perspective.

When I was given that list, the recession of 2008/2009 was still just a theoretical possibility. As of writing this, the job market is not exactly in favor of the job seekers. This raises some questions. Was the lack of focus on job security, wages and prestige just a result of a job market where unemployment was at an all-time low? Did these kids just assume that a job would always be waiting for them – and did they consequently focus on their own needs and personal development, rather than just being happy they could even GET a job? And more importantly, how does this play out globally? Is this just a local, and maybe just a temporary, phenomenon? The Top 8 list presented to me was based on a survey by CEFU, the Center for Youth Research in Copenhagen. So you would think that it would apply to Scandinavia only, right? Not at all the case. In Australia, acclaimed social researcher Mark McCrindle wrote a report on the youth of that country, *Understanding Generation Y,* in which he states:

"Indeed, when deciding to accept a job, salary ranks sixth in order of importance after training, management style, work flexibility, staff activities, and non-financial rewards. The young people of this generation do not live to work, but rather they work to live."

That exact phrase was echoed in the U.K. newspaper *The Guardian*, when they ran an article with the headline: *They don't live for work ... they work to live.* For British youth, salary took *seventh* place:

"The top priority when choosing a job was 'doing work that I love'. 'Earning lots of money' was far behind, in seventh place. When it came to walking away from an employer, a lack of motivation was the top reason followed by a work-life balance leaning too far towards the job. 'The Boomer generation [who are over 45] created the culture of long working hours and Xers [aged between 28 and 45] reluctantly accepted it,' the report said. 'But not Generation Y. While they are not work-shy, they

don't live to work. They will get the job done on time ... but on their own terms.'

So it seems it's not just a local tendency. Young people in small but rich countries like Denmark, as well as teens at large, in European industrial countries such as the United Kingdom, and across the globe in Australia, *all downplay wages* when asked about what they want in a job. Interestingly enough, the U.S. is a little different. Around the same time in 2008 as the above studies were presented, the consultancy firm Accenture examined how graduating college seniors in the U.S. viewed their job chances, and what they were looking for in a job. According to this study, *the American college grads were focused on money first.* About 87% selected the salary as *the most important characteristic in their job search.* Number two on the list are benefits, and on the number three and four spots, we find social demands such as "Interesting and challenging work," and "A social atmosphere and camaraderie with colleagues," which the other lists had at the top. Many people – including many Americans – believe that the average person in the U.S. is too money-oriented. Is the fact that the American youth entering the marketplace is so focused on wages proof of this? Fortunately it isn't the case. Rather, there seems to be a timing issue. This has to do with the Homo Conexus's work trend hitting the U.S. job market just in time for the recession of 2008-2009. But this only slowed down things a little bit. Remember back in Chapter Two when we discussed cohorts? Well, of course, there's also a cohort that's going to be impacted by the *Great Recession of 2008-2009.* At this writing, most economic experts expect the job market to bounce back in 2012. That's a four-year period, where all those in their formative years will experience some of the highest unemployment rates the U.S. has ever seen. They will not feel as secure as those who are even just a few years older. But on the other hand, those younger cohorts following them into the job market will not have been impacted in the same way.

Nobody should ever try to downplay the terrible ordeal many families have suffered as we entered the second decade of the 21st century. In some areas of the U.S., every third work-ready person was out of a job. The average unemployment rate hovered around 9-10% for the nation as a whole. With one in ten capable human beings being out of a job, it is clear that some sort of focus on job security must arise. However, this must be put into another perspective – that of *identity*. As mentioned in the previous chapter, Homo Conexus's identity is not based on the nucleus of the self-exploring the immediate surroundings. *Rather it is based on a much larger realm of beings, things and ideas, which are all networked together to make up the self.* Now try to add a place where you go for eight or more hours a day, and where you usually interact with a lot of people and ideas in order to make money. In the Industrial Age, we were very much defined by our jobs. But for Homo Conexus, the job is just another extension of the network. It's definitely an enabler. It keeps food on the table and clothes on the body, but it isn't necessarily what *defines* us. Rather, it's an exploration of a new network, and its possibilities for improving the network you already have. This hasn't changed because of the recession. Even if your job is what Douglas Coupland called a *McJob* in his book about another generation, *Generation X*, it's still a network of people that you interact with, even if you are flipping burgers or manning a toll booth. The general notion of the individual being defined by belonging to something bigger, without losing his individuality, is one of the defining differences between Homo Conexus and his or her predecessors. And if you've grown up with group dynamics and participatory culture, like Homo Conexus, it's hard to see your workplace or your family as your primary network. The decentralization megatrend forces Homo Conexus to stop placing the people he or she interacts with in a hierarchy – and basically this also means that the network you have at your place of work is not necessarily more important to defining yourself than your circle of friends, your family or even the guys you go bowling with. This is something that the recession hasn't changed. This is a megatrend that has been decades in the making, and which will continue even as job scarcity recedes.

Rise of the Freelance Nation

An interesting fact: At the height of the recession, the American workforce went freelance in droves. You would think that if job security was a bigger issue all of a sudden, freelancer numbers would be down. But it's the other way around. According to CNN, at the height of the recession, almost 30% of the active American workforce was freelancing. There are several reasons for that. One of the obvious ones is the employers' fight for survival in a tough economy. In order to stay afloat, employers would fire employees and then rehire them as freelancers, which would relieve the employers of their benefit obligations. A freelancer is cheaper because he pays for his own benefits – and he works just as hard as before, because he doesn't want to lose his job *twice.* A good chunk of the growth in the number of freelancers can definitely be attributed to this phenomenon. Another recession-related fact that helps the number of freelancers grow is the simple fact that people who are laid off will go do odd jobs, calling themselves freelancers. But the numbers speak for themselves. In June 2009, when unemployment was still on the rise, *CNN* reported that 42 million Americans were freelancing at that time. Almost a year later, in April 2010, CNN International reported that the U.S. job market had seen its fifth consecutive month of growth in the number of freelancers. That same month, the U.S. Bureau of Labor Statistics reported that the number of unemployed in the U.S. was at 15 million people. A staggering number, causing a terrible situation. But the bureau also reported that what they call "involuntary temporary workers" – meaning people who are doing odd jobs or working part-time in order to stay alive but who would rather be in a proper job position – was 9.1 million. Even if we make the bold suggestion that there are so many freelancers out there because of high unemployment, and you subtract those two numbers from the 42 million freelancers in the American workforce, the number of freelancers out there is still impressive. And it's also growing. According to projections made by WorldatWork, an association of HR executives, the U.S. could see the amount of freelancers in the workforce grow to 40% by 2019. If you add to that the health reforms passed into law in 2010, which give the self-employed access to more affordable health insurance, you have one argument less for the traditional employment situation. The freelance trend is a clear indicator of Homo Conexus entering the workforce. If your life and your identity are no longer defined by what you do, and who you work with, *but rather your ever-changing life-network*, it's a good thing to change venues once in a while. It might even be beneficial for the quality of your network. So although some studies have indicated that the 2009 recession cohort is taking a more conservative, job-security oriented approach to getting a job, the cohorts immediately before (and certainly after) probably won't. Rather, they would be defined by two current megatrends, in which the recession only made a slight dent: The rise of the freelance workforce, and the fall of the workplace as a definition of our identities. If you take a bird's-eye view of history, this cohort is going to be a small group within the Homo Conexus population.

In the Blue Corner: Industrial Man!
In the Red Corner: Homo Conexus!

In May 2008, nurses in my native Denmark went on strike for two grinding months, with unpleasant consequences for both the patients and the hospitals, the latter of which were in dire straits financially already. The argument: Nurses should be paid more – a just cause; nurses work hard. But there was a lapse of reason when the topic changed to a matter of recruitment, and about the workload being too high, because there wasn't enough man power.

As nurse Sanne Thiele wrote in a *Letter to the Editor* in the Danish newspaper *Jyllands-Posten* on May 23rd 2008, while the strike was on:

"Hospital wards all over the country are characterized by being busy and under-staffed. This poses a risk of malpractice and injuries to the patient. The working environment is under so much pressure that the nurses often return from a workday frustrated, because they haven't been able to give the best possible care.

One reason for this is that there aren't enough hands. We have difficulty recruiting and maintaining a qualified faculty. I think my colleagues and I are doing a fine and meaningful job. Why aren't we being rewarded?"

It's a classic example of how decision makers and opinion makers at the top of society have difficulty understanding Homo Conexus. If you look at the rise of the Freelance Nation, and how people prioritize network expansion over job security and salaries in the western world as described above, it becomes clear that the nurses' union execs were wrong. Young people weren't shying away from becoming nurses because of the wage level. It was because of a lack of possibilities for self-development and expanding of one's network. Even though there is huge interaction with lots of people when you are a nurse, many of the people you treat leave the hospital after a short while, and a hospital is not a place where you can move to another position within "the company" as a nurse. You can take on more (or less) administrative work, and you can switch between different medical departments. But how do you evolve? It doesn't get much easier to get into medical school, just because you're a trained nurse (although maybe it should). And in general there aren't many new avenues to explore, once you're a nurse. If anything, Homo Conexus wants opportunities, and new roads to take. And being a nurse is for life, unless you completely change directions. The Danish nurses got their raise

– which is good. But it isn't likely to buy them more manpower. Not as long as the profession is a dead end when it comes to network development and personal evolution. This isn't easy to accommodate – some jobs will be routine-like and some company structures just *have* limited room for self-development. But there's no use in trying to stop the tidal wave of progress. A Scandinavian IT trade organization executive told me that the IT trade was taking the bull by the horns. I had just proposed exchanging workers between companies, for one or two years at a time, in order to offer them a change and a possibility of expanding their networks, while they were still on a contract. But I was told that IT professionals were already doing this. Some companies were experimenting with employee exchange programs, where two people with the same skills would swap places for a while. Not just within the same company, but between companies. A kind of job rotation, where the worker simply goes to work at another company.

There's something about "Open, Sesame"

This presents a great challenge. What about the company's classified information? What about the risk of losing the employee, because the rivaling company is a better-feeling place to be? What about the risk of exchanging a good worker for a bad one? What about the competitive advantage in all the experience the employee suddenly takes to the other company? All these are valid questions. But as the anecdote at the beginning of this chapter might suggest, business secrets just aren't what they used to be. Homo Conexus grew up in a society that is much more free than the one the industrial person grew up in. In IT it's gradually becoming more popular to reveal the source code of the company's popular programs so that others may add on to them, and make them even more user friendly and popular. It started with the underground-like *Open Source* movement which is main stream today. But even big, established companies are now opening up for private users to further develop software. Even giants like Nokia and Apple have opened up. They both allow individual users with programming skills to make programs for their phones. Even the bitterest opponent of revealing how its programs work, Microsoft, is beginning to open up for consumers to further develop its products. At the other end of the product spectrum is LEGO, which has included users in the development of its products, and turned a company crisis around and made itself a smashing success. You will read more about this in Chapter Ten. Homo Conexus grew up in this more open world.The inherent decentralization which is a general theme for this book, also means that it's increasingly harder to succeed in the Network Society, if one considers one's product or company an impenetrable fort, which must be defended and hidden from the sight of others. Not a popular trait to Homo Conexus, the future client and the future employee. It's also connected to the idea of the hub. Homo Conexuses gravitate towards hubs because they trust that these centers will enhance their progress. But if the hub only sends Homo Conexus to places that are beneficial to the hub, then Homo Conexus is missing out on a plethora of opportunities – and that is against the nature of the network person who constantly seeks opportunities in the network, and who is being avalanched by new possibilities all the time. It's too obvious. It runs through the whole nine yards, the way Homo Conexuses seek information from the media, the friends they choose to have, the way they look at their profession. The reason Google became so popular is because their search engine searched all of the internet, unlike previous engines like Yahoo and AltaVista, which could search only pages they had already visited. But with Google's universal reach, web surfers didn't miss out on any possibilities. This forced Yahoo to change horses in midstream and become an ordinary search engine instead of the catalogue of websites that made it big in the 1990s. The same principle is true when it comes to Homo Conexus' social behavior. If you "ping" a friend, as described in the last chapter, and the friend only pings back when it is convenient for him or her, then the network connection isn't good – and it will eventually die. The same goes for the companies Homo Conexuses wish to work in. If it is too obvious that the company withholds development possibilities from Homo Conexus, it's no wonder that Homo Conexus looks for other pastures. This means that companies in the future may very likely be trapped between the risk of losing a little of their classified information (but in return gaining some from the rivaling companies), and the risk of losing a good employee. A cost-benefit analysis will usually show that in a society where openness is the trend (the Network Society's easy access to information makes it hard for things to be otherwise) it usually makes more sense to keep the good employee, and be willing to partly unveil how the company works. So there's no reason to fear unveiling business secrets, even during a job exchange between companies. Because, as like there's some risk in sending an employee to work for another business, *it would eventually happen anyway.* If a company doesn't provide enough challenges and personal growth possibilities for Homo Conexus, they're out the door, ready to take their experiences from the company to the competition. It's important to remember that to Homo Conexus, life is one big journey through the network. And input is coming in constantly – the equivalent of 56,000 books per day. It would be weird if Homo Conexus wasn't aware of there being better possibilities for development somewhere else than where he or she is working. And remember that it isn't just a fluke that there must be ongoing challenges and opportunities for self-realization in the job. It's the whole idea.

Death to the hierarchy

It seems that Homo Conexus is more concerned with nurturing the network than with avoiding stress. Homo Conexus seems willing to work hard – provided the result is an expansion of his or her network. No wonder, because that way work just becomes part of all the other network expansion which is constantly taking place in Homo Conexus's life. Or put differently: One of the highest priorities in Homo Conexus's life is the expansion and development of the network in order to create new possibilities. If the job helps this process then that's a good thing, and it

104

motivates Homo Conexus to perform. This is an important lesson for managers who are looking to hire members of the network generation in coming years. And managers should be aware that working for a prestigious company brand is no longer necessarily a selling point for Homo Conexus. These years, much focus is on employer branding – how businesses can use branding techniques and methods to attract the right talent. But if tomorrow's HR managers want to attract Homo Conexus, they need to examine how their company's organizational structure is laid out, and not least how to communicate this to potential new talent. You see, network-structures aren't hierarchical. They are evenly organized as heterarchies. There are points that have more gravity than others. But as a rule of thumb there is no up and down in a network – there is *in* and, to a great extent, *out*.

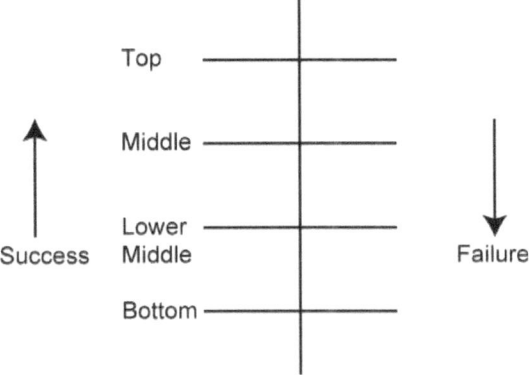

The measure of success in the Industrial Society is based on up and down.

To Homo Conexus the measure of success is rather a question of adding a third dimension. Outward.

To Homo Conexus there isn't much meaning in the sayings "climb the ladder" or "rise through the ranks." The thought of moving upward in a company doesn't make sense if the business is organized in a network. In Industrial Society logic, it's a given that those upper layers are inaccessible. And that the next step isn't possible unless one acquires knowledge, responsibility or authority. But Homo Conexus has a far more pragmatic approach to the task: What if it takes access to the upper rungs on the company ladder to solve the problem? Or what if one is in a position on that ladder that makes it hard to reach *downward*? Job prestige becomes a hollow value for Homo Conexus if it doesn't make it possible to expand the network. It's in the expansion of the network that one acquires the tools necessary to meet the challenges that arise. Therefore it's no use that parts of that network are cut off because of as personal a value as "prestige." As discussed elsewhere in this volume, the internet was created based on the principle of a tele-network capable of surviving the loss of its "center" (for example if it was bombed). Because the network is inherently decentralized, message would find their recipients anyway, through some other channel in the system. Homo Conexus solves problems in the same way. The Network Society offers so many ways of overcoming obstacles, that any point in the network can simply be "bypassed" if it is (for example) too "prestigious" to be accessible. The notion of prestige hasn't vanished from the Network Society. It's just that there are so many different networks and communities that one can gain prestige in, that there is no longer any one universal code for prestige. The status symbols of the Industrial Society – fancy cars, big houses, gold-lined no-limit credit cards – are interesting only to a fraction of Network Society inhabitants. To others, it may be just as prestigious to have 5,000 friends on Facebook. Or that your avatar in *World of Warcraft* has high status among other players. Or that the pictures of the old sports car that you tricked out beyond compare, are being circulated to fans of sports cars around the globe via the internet. Homo Conexus organizes in communities of interest, and it is within these communities that "prestige" enters the picture. Compared to this it is utterly unimportant to have prestige in the workplace. Many will probably read this and recognize the tendencies or at least think: "It's been like that for a long time." But that isn't the case. We only have to go back to the 1990s to find a fundamentally different way, among young people, of looking at professional life. Back then, it was still way more cool to work in the television industry than work at Burger King. Today, you can have a gazillion fans of your music online while making a living flipping burgers, and not letting the latter define you. For Homo Conexus, a life of prestige is no longer tied to work of any kind, but to the sum of your network.

Homo Conexus versus Industrial Man – values in the work place

There are fundamental differences in Homo Conexus's approach to professional life compared to that of the Industrial Person. As in the case of the nurses mentioned above, the times ahead are likely to bring conflict to the workplace whenever the old system tries to accommodate a new type of person, a new type of employee. Consequently, the interaction of Homo Conexus in professional life is one of the areas that is subject to extensive research. The youngest segment of the Homo Conexus bunch have been called "digital natives" by Marc Prensky, as described earlier in this book. This group is of particular interest to researchers who like to see their research being put to practical use. By performing many different studies of these digital natives, researchers hope to be able to give employers the tools they need. Which makes them able to recruit, maintain and get the best from the digital natives without triggering changes in the company's organization - and without creating conflict between them and the majority of Industrial People still toiling away in the workplaces of the Western world. One researcher who has traveled a long way down this path is Karine Barzilai-Nahon. She is head of the Center for Information and Society, and Assistant Professor at the University of Washington in Seattle. Her team is charting the differences between Industrial Society and Network Society people. In April of 2008 she unveiled some of the preliminary results. In her report *The Organizational Impact of Digital Natives: How Organizations are Responding to the Next Generation of Knowledge Workers*, presented at an information management conference in Dubai, Barzilai-Nahon and her two colleagues, Nancy Lou and Robert Mason, introduce the following table:

Values, Attitudes, and Styles	Digital Natives	Baby Boomers
Work Style	Multitasking	Time management
Learning Style	Learn from experience	Learn from instruction
Collaboration	Collaborative	Independent
Motivations	Positive reinforcement	Competition
View on Authority	Respect for others is earned	Respect for authority
Structure	Decentralized, non-hierarchical, inclusive	Centralized, hierarchical, exclusive
Information Access	Access for all	Access to those in power

The difference between Homo Conexus and Industrial Man can hardly be described more clearly, at least not when it comes to their professional life. Whereas Homo Conexus can work at many different things simultaneously without losing his or her concentration, the Industrial Person (in this model called the *Baby Boomer Generation*, those born just after World War II) is more comfortable with doing one thing at a time, and divides time accordingly. Homo Conexus is so used to seeking information, which is a constant activity – also when not working – that learning becomes a mixture of personal experiences and self-education based on the experiences of others. One trusts the knowledge of one's peers as well as that of the experts. The Industrial Person, however, maintains the centralistic way of life, with its inherent acceptance of authority. One trusts that knowledge is accumulated by individual experts, who then give directions regarding what is necessary to know. Because Homo Conexus considers himself connected to others, collaboration is a logical and preferred activity. That doesn't mean that Homo Conexus can't work independently. It just means that he or she doesn't have a problem including others (or the experience of others) into his or her work. This is unlike the Industrial Person, who was brought up to perform in order to rise through the ranks in competition with other Industrial People. Therefore one often sees Industrial People still keeping secrets – even in supposed collaborations – and making sure everyone knows about their independent performance in the middle of all the teamwork. So, even in collaborative environments, the industrial person often *competes*.

This is evident when we look at the difference in motivating factors for the two types of humans. If competition drives the Industrial Person, then positive affirmation drives Homo Conexus. As mentioned earlier, a great deal of the strength in a network is *that one doesn't stand alone.* A great part of Homo Conexus's identity is simply the sum of his or her network. In this environment, positive affirmation or stimulation is germane to the process. The idea: If everyone supports each others' projects, and makes the resources of individual networks accessible to each other, then everybody gains more. This new way of thinking is currently revolutionizing and redefining the American workplace, where this new, group-oriented dynamic is gradually edging out the traditional, outmoded, individual-focused, competitive environment. According to Barzilai-Nahon, Mason and Lou, competition is also the reason why Industrial Man would like to limit access of information to a few "power people." This is consistent with the respect for authority and hierarchy typical of Baby Boomers. In a competitive environment, it is logical and self-supportive to keep useful information from others. This is the precise opposite of the openness that Network People demand in their workplace.

Knowledge *Was* Power

One time-honored dictum holds that "knowledge is power." Those who have knowledge thereby also have power. This corresponds closely with the fact that Industrial People who cling to centralized, hierarchical structures also try to limit access to information. In the Industrial Society this would secure authority and power, which meant means of action in the old society. But things have changed. First, it has grown increasingly difficult, if not impossible, to keep a secret in the Network Society. The flow of information is so powerful that it will rip even the most tightly held information from those who cling to it. When information becomes spread out, then power also becomes spread out, and centralistic structures must give way to decentralized ones. This spreading-out of knowledge, and the growth of a decentralized social structure, is something the Network Person takes for granted, because it was never different throughout his or her upbringing. If someone is withholding information, then it's just a matter of getting that information somewhere else. If the music business won't set music free without all sorts of copyright protection, well, OK, then it's just a matter of finding that music free somewhere else. If one can't buy an encyclopedia which is frequently updated, but has to buy a new one time and again, then it's just a matter of using the free Wikipedia on the internet. If a computer game is out in the U.S. but not in Japan, and you're a Japanese gamer desperately wanting that game, you simply order it via a c/o address in the U.S. – these can be bought on the internet. Or you simply download an illegal copy. Simple fact: Homo Conexus will simply get the information he or she needs. This must eventually force companies to reconsider their distribution of power, and the structure of their organizations. And now, when the digital natives are en route to the workplace in a really big way, there is hardly any sense in thinking *more* hierarchy and *more* centralization!

Work and leisure were never separate

The last couple of years have seen much debate about whether the advent of the Network Society and online preferences will mean that borders will vanish between professional life and leisure time. On one side are the people who think that such a fusion will cause a stress epidemic. On the other side are those who call it the thinking of the Industrial Society. But not many have looked at things from the viewpoint of Homo Conexus. To the Network Person, work and leisure *were never separate*. The job is just another way for Homo Conexus to define him or her self. Therefore, it is contrary to the nature of the Network Person to be denied the possibility of communicating with the rest of his or her network, whether at home or at work. A classic error of Industrial Society is for the workplace *to try to limit* who workers may communicate with during working hours (this still occurs in far too many companies). The debate becomes too generalized when work and leisure are set up as opposites, in the context of an entire labor market. To some, communication with friends and colleagues during working hours is of the essence. For instance, graphic designers may need this communication in order to find material needed for the job. What damage is done when a mechanic answers a text message in between the adjustments he makes to a car? It isn't likely to slow down the job significantly. But it is catastrophic to the level of service if a salesperson text messages in front of customers, or is too busy with a messaging application to be helpful or even attentive. It doesn't make sense to speak of a fusion of work and leisure at a construction site, where the various workers must by definition depend upon the work of others. You may sometimes have to work extra hard to get a job done, but that's a question of overtime, not a fusion of work and leisure. The talk of a fusion between work and leisure is typically something that occurs among people who work with computers on a daily basis. They always have the possibility of taking some work home. This is more difficult for a carpenter, unless he chooses to use his spare time for work. And is also willing to lug lumber and tools to his home. But that would just mean that he would be working a lot. It wouldn't be a fusion of work and leisure. The fusion of work and leisure makes sense in the case of work "interrupting" the spare time, like answering a phone call about work related things after working hours. Or replying to work e-mails when checking private e-mails. In most cases, work is invading spare time. But what about the opposite – when leisure invades work? In my opinion, Homo Conexus introduces another development to the workplace. Because one's profession is only a part of the network, Homo Conexus feels a part of, it never leaves his mind. But on the other hand, leisure doesn't leave his mind when at work either. For the Network Person who has assignments that can be dealt with using a computer or telephone, it isn't unnatural to take care of them at home, after working hours. Just as Homo Conexus has no qualms about using 15 minutes to pay bills online while at work. In this case the Industrial Person is different, because the entire industrialization and the construction of the Welfare State in the first half of the 20th century was based on a division between home and work. As futurologist Jesper Bo Jensen, Ph.D., puts it in an article on his home page:

"In Industrial Society the division between work and leisure became clearly defined. The time at work was working hours and the time outside work was leisure time. The spare time could be used for recreational purposes, so one could go back to work.

The notion of work and the division of life into working hours and spare time meant a clear classification of human relations. Colleagues (work buddies) belonged to the working hours while family belonged to the spare time. In the same way there was a physical split-up between the workplace and the home. In earlier times work had taken place in and around the home, but with the industrialization the work moved out into the workplaces (i.e. factories).

In this way family and home became separate from work..."

This is a quite precise description of the world of Industrial Man – as it was passed on to him in those founding years where he was defined as a cohort. But this isn't the world that Homo Conexus grew up in. Colleagues, friends and family are all part of the same network to Homo Conexus. In Homo Conexus's world, recreation is a part of the working hours. He wouldn't think twice about playing a quick online game to clear his mind, even though this may come off as laziness, irresponsibility or worse to the Industrial Person. But then Homo Conexus would have no problem spending equivalent time on a work-related problem should his boss call him late at night. Note that there is a reciprocal effect. If the Network Person isn't free to let leisure affect work, then naturally he or she isn't inclined to let work affect leisure. But before Homo Conexus reaches that point he would most likely have moved on to a place that better understands what the Network Society is all about.

No stress

One might think that Homo Conexus would get all stressed out by work cutting into his free time. But there are two very important issues here. One is fact that Homo Conexus simply doesn't *think* the way Industrial Man does. It seems that the "digital native" brain simply works differently. And the other is the fact that there is a difference between work/life balance and work/life networks. Let's examine the Homo Conexus brain first. We've already dealt with the fact that the technological networks we see all around us are actually structured in the same way that our brain cells are. So what's the difference? Marc Prensky argued, back when he introduced the idea of the digital natives, that there was a different way of *thinking* which applied to them. He believes that the massive influence from computer-games during Homo Conexus's entire upbringing has brought a sharpening of the attention as a result of several hours of daily "training." He writes:

"Several hours a day, five days a week, sharply focused attention—does that remind you of anything? Oh, yes - video games! That is exactly what kids have been doing ever since Pong arrived in 1974. They have been adjusting or programming their brains to the speed, interactivity, and other factors in the games, much as boomers' brains were programmed to accommodate television, and literate man's brains were reprogrammed to deal with the invention of written language and reading (where the brain had to be retrained to deal with things in a highly linear way)"

Prensky points to a statement made by William D. Winn, leader of the learning centre at the Human Interface Technology Laboratory at the University of Washington. He believes that children that grew up with computers

"...think differently from the rest of us. They develop hypertext minds. They leap around. It's as though their cognitive structures were parallel, not sequential."

This hypertextuality is characteristic to Homo Conexus's way of thinking. In order to contain the large amount of network input, Homo Conexus must develop a way of multi-tasking, and a *parallel* way of understanding connections instead of a serial one. In relation to work this means that to some it is possible to be at work but to think about leisure simultaneously without becoming stressed. Something points in the direction that Homo Conexus's preferred work life is one that has a natural decentralized balance between time spent at work, and time spent on leisure. The points in time and specific locations mean less to Homo Conexus – as is also the case with so many other factors. The important thing is the distribution of time, and the freedom to navigate throughout one's entire network. The latter also means removing the barriers between your personal network and your professional one. Most people today have their professional network on sites like LinkedIn or Plaxo, while their personal networks are maintained on Facebook. That's changing. As more people become freelancers, and have to leverage their personal network all the time, they stop making those distinctions. This is why Homo Conexus gets upset when an employer limits access to Facebook at work, a current trend among larger companies, which exist enmired in the delusion that spending work time on Facebook somehow reduces productivity.

It's actually the exact opposite!

Rob Cross is a professor at University of Virginia, held in high regard as one of the primary experts on implementing networks in the workplace. He is a champion and promoter of ONA – *Organizational Network Analysis.* With this effective tool, Cross and his team has done studies of several major corporations, mapping out who answers to whom; which interpersonal relations people in the organizations have; even who gets together privately outside the workplace. The analysis also paints a picture of where different capabilities and competences reside in the organization, *regardless* of titles or where these competences are *supposed* to be placed. It often provides a clear image of a corporation, one that reveals many low-hanging fruits that can be picked at once, where much productivity can be won immediately. One place to start is with the hubs. There are always some people who are more connected to one another than to others by shared competencies or personal relations. But if these people are not given the time and opportunity to act as hubs, but rather are just asked to "do their job" (whatever that function is), they become bottlenecks in the flow of information through the organization. Everyone will come to them for answers, and they will become overloaded. And even though Homo Conexus might have a better way of thinking when it comes to handling this type of load, everyone has a breaking point. But by either dispersing that person's competencies, capabilities throughout the network or by empowering that person as a hub (by relieving him of some non-network-based tasks), Cross actually finds that productivity and efficiency rise dramatically. ONAs also reveal unproductive "silos," where groups of people huddle together around a product or a task, obtaining or creating valuable information which should be spread throughout the organization – but isn't. This insularity problem can even be traced to one person, who might on the outside *seem* very sociable and placed physically among all the other people in the office. But when you look at the network, that person's assets might not be put to good use because he or she uses them *only* for the exact tasks at-hand, never sharing the information and knowledge obtained by solving the problems.

Cross also sees hierarchical structure in corporations as a thing of the past, and presses for a more decentralized company structure. He writes:

"Networks can be biased by an over-reliance on people who occupy certain hierarchical positions. Managing relationships with those higher than, at the same level, and lower than you is a hallmark of a well-rounded organizational network. In general, balance is important, and people's networks seem to fall out of balance when they don't maintain enough relationships overall, when they focus too heavily on those higher in the organization, or when they miss the technical expertise that can often be gained from those at lower levels."

Now add Facebook to this whole discussion. Into this hodgepodge of social relations and formal/informal distinctions, comes this tool that crosses all the usual social borders. People of all ages, cultures, colors and creeds are on Facebook. Some are Homo Conexuses and some aren't. According to a webzine for leaders in the technology sector, CIO.com, trying to ban Facebook is a losing battle anyway, since people will then turn to their smartphones or other means of getting online, in order to maintain their private social network. But banning social networks in the workplace also means shutting out a huge resource. Imagine having a panel of hundreds of people at your disposal to reach out to when you're in doubts about something – and not using them? Not only is banning social networks bad HR policy when it comes to attracting talent from the Homo Conexus pool. It also cuts off the individual employee from a huge informational resource. And then there's the inter-organizational effect. As Rob Cross teaches us, informal networks are really important in the workplace. In fact, *it might be where all your productivity lies, and you wouldn't even know it,* because you are focused on the formal, hierarchical structure. How do you strengthen the informal ties between employees? This may seem really trivial, but it's true – you help them get to know each other better. Many companies spend gazillions of dollars each year on "team building" efforts – while at the same time shutting down access to the one website where their employees could learn about each others' common leisure interests and hobbies: Facebook! It just seems silly and totally in conflict with the wish to strengthen informal relations within an organization, thereby creating coherence, more efficient information flow and higher productivity. Many companies use "security concerns" as an excuse; that allowing access to social networks would mean opening the door to outsiders who are not as benign as you would wish. Malware like viruses, trojans and spyware would flood the internal network! However, this hasn't happened in the corporations who *allow* sites like Facebook. And the reason is, of course, that you can easily limit the download of malignant files without limiting the access to a website. Then there's the question of critical or proprietary information flowing out of the company. Well, you can never safeguard yourself against this anyway. First of all, as mentioned earlier in this chapter, openness in a company is a factor which many Homo Conexuses will consider when choosing a job. And second, if you shut down access to Facebook, it would also be good idea only to hire people who don't drink and who sit in their rooms in all their leisure time, only to come out when it's time to work again. That's probably what Apple's Steve Jobs wished he had done when the fourth generation model of the iPhone was prematurely revealed online because one of Apple's employees left it at a bar in Silicon Valley. However, Apple ended up selling three million iPhone 4s in only three weeks, because of the hype generated by that premature revelation. This happened even though the AntennaGate scandal exploded, and Jobs had to call a press conference to dispel rumblings about bad reception on the iPhone 4. He owes a great deal to one beer-happy Apple employee. And yet large corporations still do it. Two examples where this misguided strictness borders on the idiotic is the large Hollywood record company (which shall remain nameless, suffice to say that it is one of the so-called Majors) who has banned access to MySpace. MySpace, although it is being deserted fast, has been *the* venue for discovering new talent as well as for established bands to connect with their fans. And yet this record company, due to its ties to an even larger corporation, did not allow access to MySpace. There's also the example of the American/Swedish publishing house Bonnier, who got much (bad) publicity in Scandinavia, because they also limited their employees' access to Facebook. This is a company whose publications include magazines that rely heavily on a steady information flow from the outside world. And yet they shut down access to one of their employees' biggest sources of information and inspiration.

How to ...

It's easy enough to criticize the more conservative way of handling these things. So let's get practical:

According to *The Organized Impact of Digital Natives* by Barzilai-Nahon, Lou and Mason, there are three ways in in which companies typically react to these new demands by Homo Conexus in the workplace. There is the cautionary way, the responsive way and the proactive way. According to the report, the cautionary company will typically think that its structure is good as it is, and will probably limit the employees' access to Instant Messaging clients, private e-mail systems or Facebook. The responsive company knows that there are changes coming. Often times it is a company of some size in which progressive elements are trying to implement change in the hope of preventing damages caused by the conflicts that invariably arise as more and more Homo Conexuses join the work force. According to the report, "these progressive elements" are weighing the pros and cons of introducing new technologies and complying with Homo Conexus's demand for possibilities of broadening their networks in the workplace - and they make the decisions on the fly, at such a rate that conflicts arise.

The proactive companies are usually ahead of the game. They may be owned by one or more Homo Conexuses. Or maybe their product is dependent on methods that only a network person can bring to the table. However, the authors of the report stress that there are many examples of established companies that choose to be proactive in this respect. It can seem overwhelming to the manager of a company to take all this into consideration when preparing for a new generation of workers. But the following examples give some hands-on suggestions (in no particular order):

Rethink the company's internal communication

Stop using e-mail. A lot of companies today are based on e-mail-communication. In some places it's practical because e-mail is an easy way of archiving dialog either for subsequent analysis or security reasons. But to Homo Conexus, e-mail is ye olde school. It was invented in the early 1970s and is nothing new to the digital natives. On the contrary, it's old-fashioned. As you will read later in this book, convenience and instant gratification are incredibly important to Homo Conexus when they use media or consume everyday products. In this context, e-mail is just too primitive, and often also too slow. According to a survey from 2006, commissioned by the E.U., only an average of 50% of the young people surveyed reported that they even had an e-mail address. Further, most of those that had one used it primarily for schoolwork. Since then, *Pew Internet* and *American Life Project* concluded that only 16 percent of American youth used e-mail. Communication must be easy and swift, and the conversation can be ongoing. Therefore, *instant messaging is a better way of communicating internally than e-mail*. It's harder to ignore, and it is still possible to log the conversation.

Think in decentralized organizational structures

A level company setup is not a particularly ground-breaking thought; neither is accessibility and the spread of knowledge. But there are still companies which organize themselves in strict hierarchical structures, be it for traditional or ego-driven reasons. These companies will most likely face great difficulty in the years ahead, when they must deal with dissatisfied Homo Conexuses, that's if they can even recruit the manpower they need.

CEO: Don't manifest your position of power because you want a cool car

When professional prestige leaves the workplace, some of the "envy value" goes with it. But some managers still manifest their position of power to the employees, because they think this makes them indispensable, and that this behavior will secure leadership privileges – like status symbols of the Industrial Society. In other words: some managers, and mid-level managers, use every chance to flash their power, so that people understand why they deserve the nice company car and the large pay-check. But this means keeping an outfit, or an entire company, locked into Industrial Society thinking. OK, Homo Conexuses also can be envious of cool car, but that doesn't make the owner of the car a more *authoritative* person. Homo Conexus doesn't care about prestige. So using prestige as a means to gain respect within a company is bound to fail in the Network Society.

Spend resources on breaking the fall

When things are set in motion to change the company in order to greet Network People as employees, the Industrial Society people start to get anxious. And with good reason. All of a sudden they must compete with multi-tasking geniuses, who may even understand technology better than the bosses do. Conflicts will arise in the workplaces when the Industrial Person must learn to understand why it is OK to let Homo Conexus spend 30 minutes killing aliens on the internet. It isn't obvious that Homo Conexus *is also still working* when everyone else has punched out for the day. Or that Homo Industrialis still has a lot to offer in terms of maturity and greater focus. Bridges need to be built. Create networking groups with both types of people in them and motivate them to utilize each others' strengths while working with the task at hand. Big changes within a company are always difficult, especially when they deal with psychology, or when there are generation or culture gaps to bridge. Spend your resources on making this process as humane as possible – it pays in the end.

Be happy for the swifter communication and higher efficiency

Believe it or not, it is in your best interest when Homo Conexus is in a meeting and is sending a text message, or sending a reply on Messenger, and still seems to be 100% concentrated on what is going on in the room. *This multi-tasking is natural for them.* Instead of letting it bother you, you should be happy that you have an employee who delivers simultaneous three-layered communication, and therefore is more efficient than you're actually paying him to be. Up until now it hasn't been customary to pay higher salaries to people who can multi-task, has it? On the contrary, you should encourage multi-tasking by molding the company, or any specific work function, after the person who can multi-task. Don't limit Homo Conexus' multi-channel communication – it would mean only using a fraction of a persons abilities.

***

CHAPTER SEVEN:
HOMO CONEXUS AND SOCIETY

Until now we have dealt with how Homo Conexus is a human with many different biological networks; how Homo Conexus's identity is shaped; and how he or she goes to work. But one of the areas, which have been subject to the most attention when speaking of human networks, has been in the field of sociology – how we network together. Thousands of books have been written on this subject – most of them bursting with methods for using "your network" to get a better job, or achieve some other form of success. But it's a question whether it even makes any sense to speak of "having" a network. Homo Conexus is rather defined by its entering into a network *which already exists*. It can seem absurd to speak of "ownership" of a network which undergoes massive changes when it has moved a couple of connections down the line, changes about which the person, the "owner," can do absolutely nothing. If it is at all possible to be "in charge" of one's network, this would only be the case when it comes to the closest connections. This is something a number of researchers have looked into. Studies in social network theory date back to the 1800s. But it has only been in the last 50 years that discussions have really flourished, and around 2003 a regular avalanche of books was published about how the world is set up in networks. Two outstanding examples are Albert-Laszlo Barabási's *Linked* and Mark Buchanan's *Nexus*. The beginning of the 2000s is a pivotal point due to the new possibilities for accessing data. Until then it had been difficult to create networks that were big and stable enough to collect sufficient data on network connections to allow for scientific research. There had been many theories, some backed by more crude methods than others. It wasn't until the internet became popular with the masses in the middle of the 1990s that this tool for collecting data on network connections became so effective that it could be statistically useful. Suddenly networks could be charted, and their changes studied which allowed for mathematical models for network theory – followed by comparisons to real life. It was around the turn of the Millennium that comparative studies became possible between these models and the way we live, which in turn, years later, has led to the book you're now reading. There are some key players who are always brought into the picture when we look at the sociology of networks, and this is due to the research area being so new. In order to give an overall impression of Homo Conexus, this book won't make an exception. You will now hear of the man who fathered the theory of there only being six links between people in this world, of hubs, of strong and weak links in the network, and not least how humans and things can enter into a network with each other. But first we will deal with the megatrend of society which enabled the rise of Homo Conexus, who lives and breathes for the creation of networks; in a word: *decentralization*.

The decentralization megatrend

Have you gone from using a big bank to using a smaller one recently? Or used Skype as an alternative to calling from an ordinary phone? Have you recently quit your job to work freelance? Or started shopping in separate stores instead of a big box warehouse, or maybe you've been spending more money at the local kiosk than at the supermarket? Have you recently bought a Nintendo Wii, Playstation 3 or an Xbox 360, even though you already own a game console? If you can answer any one of these questions positively, you're most likely a part of one of the megatrends that characterize the transition into the Network Society, namely that of *decentralization*. The Network Society is becoming increasingly decentralized. No wonder, really, if we take Paul Baran's theory (Chapter Three) into consideration. If we humans in Network Society behave like packets on the internet, then we are in fact decentralized. Paul Baran's structure of network communications disposed of the need for centrals, in order to make any network more sturdy. In much the same way there's a growing trend in our society right now which tears down the big centers, leveling society out. Megatrends are trends which don't just come and go with the changing of the seasons, but change society fundamentally, in all its aspects, over the course of time. Decentralization is a just such a megatrend, and it started when the first Homo Conexuses were born. Now it has really gained momentum, not least due to the recent financial crisis. But decentralization is nothing new. The world has previously witnessed major centralizations which have subsequently been wound down by a trend of decentralization. Take, for instance, the Roman Empire, which was a massive centralization of power over most of Europe – and parts of North Africa and the Levant – all concentrated in a single Italian city. When centralization becomes as grand as it was under Roman dominance, it is hard to maintain for various reasons: It is difficult to exercise close control as the distance grows between the center and the edge of the network. As Paul Baran discovered when studying telenetworks, centralization makes the whole system vulnerable. If the head is decapitated, the body will follow. And indeed the unraveling of the Roman Empire happened as a slow decentralization. First, Rome lost its status as the Emperor's home town. Then the empire was split into a Western and an Eastern Roman Empire, subject to an ever increasing number of attacks from local rivals until Rome's great power eventually crumbled away. A more contemporary example is the organization of Europe after World War II. In the postwar years a welfare state was introduced in most Northern European countries, where the state, the federal government, exercised central ownership of nationwide structures. The state owned the telephone network; all public transportation; the power companies. Indeed, in many European countries it wasn't until the early 1980s that private radio and TV broadcasting became legal. This centralization was a powerful tool for getting Europe back on its feet after the war. But the Continent has since become subject to gradual decentralization. And that decentralization peaks in Network Society. In this respect, decentralization is not to be understood as a political term. It doesn't necessarily bring about privatization and deregulation, which are typical right wing political goals. The health care reforms passed by President Obama's administration in 2010 is an example of how the government intervenes to create a more diverse marketplace by decentralizing access to health insurance. Where you would previously get it from your employer or by yourself, the new laws create more private health care providers, and mandate that everyone gets insurance. This means that health insurance itself is decentralized from the "center" of the workforce, and distributed among the general population. And this is done through slightly *more* regulation. Another example is found in the E.U., whose trade laws mandate that products cannot be sold exclusively in one country, but must be made available to the entire union. This is also decentralization mandated through regulation. It's everywhere right now. The elements of society which refuse to comply with this megatrend will be increasingly worse off as the Homo Conexus population grows. In Chapter Six I mentioned the problems unions were facing with recruiting members. This is what happens when one centralizes an organization in a world where people think decentralized. The same goes for the workplaces that become less and less hierarchical, and where power is consequently decentralized. There are many other examples. During the recent financial crisis the world has witnessed a flurry of consolidations. A number of American financial giants have been forced to merge, or buy one another, in order to survive. And many mid-sized companies are letting themselves be bought by giants just to stay in business. But aren't these consolidations really centralizations of power within the market? Not necessarily. Mergers and consolidations don't mean the simple taking over of the market shares of the merging partner. As the mergers within the telecommunications industry showed earlier this year, it takes a considerable amount of resources to make consolidations work. Company cultures need to merge.

People need to be fired and others hired. Properties need management. Often the results of a consolidation aren't visible

126

until years after the fact, and after a period of great turmoil, personally and financially. On top of this, a financial crisis has often been the forerunner of a consolidation, as is exactly the case in the present financial environment. During such a crisis the partners may have already lost a number of market shares. Shares which aren't automatically recouped by a merger – and then there's all the monetary value that evaporates with the pulling out of shareholders, investors and customers who may not like the consolidation. This creates a net effect which usually means more space in the marketplace during a time of mergers and consolidations. Smaller players get the chance of going for the market shares the mergers have opened up. In other words, a period of mergers gives rise to many new, smaller enterprises which help to balance out what may look like a centralization of the market into fewer entitities. As they're allowed to grow bigger, the market becomes *decentralized* instead. This also goes for the level of recruitment. Many companies use more freelancers at the rate that an increasingly larger part of the workforce chooses to become freelancers. This is a decentralization of the labor market, which takes place as a result of decentralization in the market as a whole. This tendency towards emancipation from the "silos," the big centers, is a mechanism which is seminal to the trend of decentralization. Futurologist Rolf Jensen, who has advised corporations from Korea to the U.S., and is hailed as one of the fathers of the concept of the Experience Economy, has pointed to the trend of decentralization for quite some time. This was even before network research emerged to make us aware that we're *en route* to a new stage in human evolution. He called it "individualization." We now know that what may come off as an ego-centered "individualization" inherent in Network Society, is really just the marking of one's presence in the greater community – the network – with the intention of acquiring more network connections. Jensen didn't take this into consideration when he produced a report in 2006, in which he speaks of the X-theory:

"It entails that the standardized mass production is on its way out and is replaced by individually customized products. In a phase of transition the number of product varieties will increase. This happens when we are dealing with dairy products, beer and other consumer goods, and clothing. The 'Fordism,' or standardization, is a thing of the 19th century... "

One of the reasons for this tendency is, according to Jensen:

"...a decreasing acceptance of authority. We're no longer afraid of not being like the others."

But it is important not to perceive the staging of oneself as an individual as an egotistical, self-isolating process. On the contrary, one shapes one's identity in this way in order to enter into networks and be attractive to others. You find the special brand of beer that you like. You make your own *Nike* shoe on *Nike*'s homepage. You build a profile of yourself, as with social networks, and thereby strengthen your individuality. But the motivation for this is not to be a strong individual. On the contrary, the idea is to become a point in the network, which can connect to as many other points as possible, and thereby access greater possibilities for self-development. One defines one's choices in identity more clearly, because this makes it easier to find others with the same interests. I like wine from the Santa Barbara region in California, so do you – let's form a network. However, the X-theory is primarily a good example of the trend of decentralization. The lower acceptance of authority is a result of Homo Conexus being skeptical of a message even if (or perhaps because) it comes from a big, centralistic sender. We are not as interested in conformity as we used to be, because conformity is the same as centralizing your values.

But the best example of the trend of decentralization in relation to Rolf Jensen's mentioning of the X-theory is our consumer goods. Bestsellers aren't what they used to be. It used to be that there were only a few authors at a time who really sold books to the masses. Only a few movies were blockbusters. Today this image is blurred. The big rallying points have been substituted for many small centers of attention with smaller audiences. More writers, but fewer readers for every book. More movies in the theaters, but fewer moviegoers. But nowhere else has this tendency been as evident as it has in the music business.

When the music industry (nearly) died

The music industry is the perfect example of how an entire industry decentralizes from top to bottom, because of a trend of decentralization in the market. From gigantic, centralistic companies all the way down to the individual person. For most of the past century of recorded music, the music industry consisted of many different companies, with names like Columbia, CBS, RCA, Atlantic Records, Virgin, Elektra and many others. Then a period of consolidation in the 1970s and 1980s herded most of them into six giants.: Polygram, Sony Music, Universal/MCA, EMI, Warner and BMG. When crisis struck the music industry towards the end of the 1990s, due to the introduction of the CD burner and file sharing of MP3s, another period of consolidation took place over the course of a few years. Universal bought Polygram, and Sony merged with BMG. The international music business was now consolidated into just four big companies. It may have meant that it was easier for the artists to shop their product, since there weren't so many companies to deal with. But the consolidation also brought a centralistic arrogance, which in time would prove disastrous to the four giants. When, in 2002, the newly appointed international director of EMI, Alain Levy, announced the firing of 1,800 employees along with a tightening up and cutting back of the artist roster, he said: "We have streamlined the artist roster, which I found fairly bloated. For example, we had 49 artists in Finland and I don't think there are 49 Finns that can sing."

Ouch!

The inappropriateness of this gratuitous remark was magnified by the fact that EMI had an enormous market share in Finland (about 20%), because a local Finnish label had been bought. It caused an uproar throughout the industry. Since then EMI has tried to merge with Warner Music, because it simply can't make ends meet, despite representing giant catalogues like The Beatles and Pink Floyd; It's a perfect example that the workings of the fall of the Roman Empire, also can take place in the modern world: That centralization leads to a lack of knowledge of what goes on in the fringes of the network – and that it can lead to fatal errors. Meanwhile, so-called "independent" or "indie" companies that aren't associated with the four giants have taken over large parts of the market. In the U.S., the indie companies who are part of the music organization Merlin, have an 8% market share, or as much as EMI. And Merlin doesn't even represent any of the really big independent labels. LiveNation is a newish independent player in the market which has attracted big names like Madonna and R.E.M. by offering them deals that cover concert promotion and tours as well as the release of music. But the music business is experiencing even further decentralization these days. Bands use the possibilities of the internet to market their music autonomously and independently of the record label system. The internet is full of places like MySpace, Reverbnation or Garageband, allowing artists to make their music available to the public without having to go through the traditional system. And through online CD stores like CD Baby, one can release music on physical CDs without coming near Industrial Society's methods for distribution of music. Through digital music outlets like the iTunes Store or eMusic it has long been possible to buy music from artists who don't even release physical media, or even have a big label supporting them. The music business has been decentralized, and then some.

Value from the fringes

The same thing is currently happening to the movie industry. In 2002 Dylan Avery, who was 18 at the time, began investigating the background of the terrorist attacks in New York on September 11, 2001. This led to his finishing *Loose Change* in 2005, a documentary which attempts to prove that is was really the U.S. Government that was in charge of the attacks – or at least played a part. It cost around $5,000 to make, and in the beginning it was distributed free on the internet. In May, 2006 it went to the top of Google Video's list of most viewed videos. 10 million people had seen the film at that point, and since then that number has grown considerably, because the film is also being spread via bit-torrent networks and has been released on DVD. According to Wikipedia more than 40 million people have now seen the movie via Google Video, and more than a million DVDs have been sold. An unscientific but nonetheless interesting fictitious experiment: If we take a bigger film within the same genre, which has been more expensive to make, and has been distributed and marketed through the traditional channels, Michael Moore's *Fahrenheit 9/11*, then it has grossed an estimated $222 million. A DVD or a ticket to the movies costs around $10, so it would be fair to assume that 22 million people have seen the movie. Even though it is likely to have been seen by many more on TV and loaned or rented DVDs, and even though my calculation isn't scientifically perfect, it is still amazing how close *Loose Change* has come to *Fahrenheit 9/11*'s popularity without the same budget for production or marketing.

This is decentralization of the world of video showing its face. Distribution has become free, and production methods less expensive. This has paved the way for a decentralization of the movie industry – which again has led to the launching of initiatives like Indiegogo.com, where one can get movies *crowdfunded*. In other words, if you have a good documentary in the makings, but lack financing, you can upload the concept to Indiegogo, and people can then make donations. And because the community around Indiegogo is so extensive and international, we're not talking mere pebbles here. If your project captures the attention of the masses, you can have your budget in no time. Likewise, Wikipedia collected over $16 million in 2010 from people interested in keeping that *decentralized* encyclopedia on its feet. (More about this in Chapter Nine). So, even though there's a recession causing a period of consolidation, the trend of decentralization is making its mark on the market. *Short term centralizations are followed by long term decentralization*. The internet and counterculture guru Douglas Rushkoff, who gave us terms like "viral communication" and "social currency," views decentralization as more than a trend. To him, decentralization helped cause the financial crisis which erupted in 2008. I talked to him while he was waiting for delivery of a proof of his next book, which deals with the same topic. I asked him why decentralization was happening right now.

"I think these things happen right now because of the emergence of the internet, and because people now are able to create value from the periphery. In the past 400 years since, the corporation was born and married to the government, people have been robbed of the opportunity to create value for themselves. If you want to start a company, you have to borrow money. You can't just earn them on your own. This landscape is simply not made for decentralized value creation from a lot of small units. But the internet changed all that. And it had such a massive and pervasive effect on the economy that we're only now seeing the real effects of it."

Rushkoff believes that the rise of the internet and the trend of decentralization have played a big part in the great banking collapses of 2007 and 2008, collapses which started an international financial crisis. He believes that the recession:

"...is really just the second leg of the dot.com crash. We got out of that crisis by creating a speculative bubble in the real estate market and made our losses back that way. But the way value is created has changed [with the recession]. There's still a lot of value being created and a lot of money being spent, but it happens in another way, that doesn't involve so many loans. The effect of that is that the large, centralistic banks were no longer able to make money the way they were used to. I can start a computer games company or a software company without having to borrow money to build a factory – and then what are businesses who make money lending to people, going to do?"

According to Rushkoff, the decentralization has brought about such powerful changes in our economy that it led to the recent crisis. But decentralization pops its head up in many other, and less dramatic, places.

Decentralization is everywhere

From the media to the places we shop, and places we go to school and work: Our lives are steadily becoming more decentralized, which supports Paul Baran's vision of a robust network without centers. Even the gadgets in our pockets have become less centralized, although we thought they would become consolidated. For years there has been talk of media convergence, a term defining how consumer technologies would merge in order to create a few electronic devices that could do everything at once. Instead of having an MP3 player, a camera, a phone and a watch to lug around it would all be combined in one simple unit. But if we look at a report produced by the interactive marketing heavyweight Razorfish, it comes to light, that the respondents would actually like more units that did different things:

"Despite user requests for a single mobile, PC, or gaming device to do everything, we found users increasingly willing to embrace multiple devices—even when those devices possess overlapping

capabilities. For instance, a Nintendo Wii for the whimsical side of their gaming lives and an XBOX 360 for competition. A laptop for managing the business of life and another littered with stickers for fun. A smart phone for e-mail and a flip phone for weekends."

The centralization which many had expected from the convergence may end up a *decentralization* instead.

In general, the media have become more decentralized – there are more channels, and more *niche-oriented* channels, on all media platforms. Granted, some fall off the map, but the past 25 years an enormous wealth of TV channels, free newspapers, internet media and radio channels have joined the scene, whereas there used to be only a few media worth consideration. The way we behave as consumers has also become decentralized. Small convenience stores are preferred over large malls that can be difficult to get to (*See* Chapter Nine). Large central warehouse operations generally suffer financially too, and in Japan, the big warehouses – defined as warehouses that don't have individual stores – have lost market shares to specialized stores for 12 years in a row. In the area of education, decentralization is taking place as well. For years UNESCO (the UN's organization for education and culture) has recommended a strategy of decentralization to developing countries. And in the U.S., the internal organization for third world countries uses Mali, Argentina, Peru and Egypt as examples of how decentralization of the educational system has increased learning possibilities.

Our workplaces have also become more decentralized. One wouldn't think so, when you're on your morning commute into some big city and you see all the roads jammed with cars. Despite the fact that New York and Los Angeles have many corporate headquarters in their city centers, there are fewer people who actually *go to work* downtown. The Brookings

Institution, which produces analysis for political counseling in Washington, D.C., released a report in 2008 which studied the 98 largest urban areas of the U.S. It reveals that only 21% of the people living in those areas worked within a 3 mile radius. But 45% were working more than 10 miles from the city center. The survey showed that *the greater the urban area, the further people were working from the center.* This is because many companies have moved out into suburban "industrial parks" because rent in city centers has increased considerably within the past 10 years – and the recession isn't likely to make prices go down enough for the companies to move back. But most importantly, the study showed that this isn't just a passing thing, but a trend. Slowly but surely, the number of jobs in the city centers decreased from 1998 to 2006, in 95 of the 98 cities. The jobs went from the centers to the outskirts. And according to the report this was happening across the board. It wasn't just companies in need of production capacity that moved out. Generally, the number of jobs increased in the cities from 1998 to 2006. But in the centers there was a less than 1% increase, while the jobs outside the city centers went up by 17%. Clearly a trend of decentralization. But the most impressive thing about the trend of decentralization is that once you're aware of it, you will spot it everywhere. Keep it in mind the next time you watch TV, read the paper, go shopping, make investments, or have friends or family over for dinner. Decentralization is the undercurrent of Network Society – and therefore it is everywhere.
Decentralization is so important to Homo Conexus because of the need for expansion of the network. It's self evident that a centralized network has fewer options for expansion than a decentralized one. The latter is split into more, smaller entities as opposed to a centralized network, and there are simply more points to explore or to network with.

Stanley Milgram and the six degrees

Today, everyone has heard about 6 degrees of separation. It's the single most quoted experiment when people talk about networks – mostly because it found fame through the *Kevin Bacon Game,* which in turn found fame through the early days of the World Wide Web. There is good reason for this. Because if you dig a little deeper than the surface, the Milgram experiment shows us how early on the decentralization trend began. And so it's worth telling his story once again from this perspective. Until the spread of the use of the internet, Stanley Milgram was primarily known for a single, ground breaking experiment. In 1960 the Nazi Adolf Eichmann, widely considered the mastermind behind the holocaust of World War II, was captured in Argentina. His case was tried in court in Jerusalem in 1961 to great media attention – and while the world was watching, Eichmann admitted to his part in the horrible ethnic cleansing that had taken place throughout Europe. He was sentenced and hanged in 1962. During the trial Eichmann had said what other Nazis had said before him, 15 years earlier in Nuremberg: he was "just following orders." At that time Stanley Milgram was 29 years old. He had just finished his Ph.D. in psychology at Harvard, where he subsequently lectured and produced his research. Milgram was intrigued by Eichmann's defense, and decided to perform a series of experiments to look into how much pain humans were willing to subject each other to, when "just following orders." He wanted to prove that people in Industrial Society had an inherent acceptance of authority, which could make them do nearly anything if only the order and the acceptance were strong enough. The experiment created much attention and portrayed Stanley Milgram as a controversial character. It has since become one of the most famous experiments in the history of psychology. Films were made, and songs were written, about it. But as Network Society was beginning to blossom, another and far less controversial Stanley Milgram experiment turned up. For years scientists had tried to prove that the real world was as small as the mathematical models would have it be. When Marconi received the Nobel Prize for Physics in 1909, for the invention of radio, he mentioned in his acceptance speech, that he had calculated that it would take an estimated average of 5.83 connected radio stations to cover the whole world. This allegedly inspired the Hungarian Frigyes Karinthy to write a short story introducing the thought that people everywhere are only separated by the same six connections. This is known as the *Six Degrees of Separation.* In the 1950s mathematician Manfred Kochen and sociologist Ithiel de Sola Pool were working in Paris to prove this nearly mythological theory mathematically. During their work they had a visit from the young Stanley Milgram, who was fascinated by the thought. After the controversial experiments of looking into people "just following orders," he started working on what came to be known as *The Small World Problem* – the challenge of proving that the world is really rather small. The results of this new series of experiments were published in *Psychology Today* in 1967, but didn't create the kind of attention of Milgram's earlier experiments. It wasn't until the world started realizing that the internet is in fact an image of Milgram's results, that they were given any further attention. Milgram wanted to assess the probability that two randomly chosen people were connected. He sent letters primarily to Omaha, Nebraska and to Wichita, Kansas which, because of their relatively provincial locations, could be assumed to have little connection to the intellectual research environment of Boston, Massachusetts. These randomly chosen people received an information package from Milgram, in which he explained the experiment. In the enclosed letter was the name of a person in Boston. If the recipient knew this person he was to send the package to him or her directly. If not, he was to send the package to the person in his circle of acquaintances whom he considered most likely to know the person in Boston. Then, when the letters finally reached the recipient in Boston, it was clear from the list of senders how many connections it had taken to reach him or her. In some cases, packages never came through. But this didn't necessarily mean that there wasn't a connection between the first sender and the final recipient – it just meant that someone along the line had chosen not to participate in the experiment. But in many of these experiments, enough packages arrived in order for Milgram to make statistical conclusions. Some of the packages had only taken two or three connections to arrive; others had taken more like ten. But characteristically, the average number of connections it took to connect two randomly chosen people was six. Precisely as Marconi and Karinthy had predicted. In 1994, around the time when the internet became a widespread phenomenon, these thoughts emerged once again due to the busy life of actor Kevin Bacon. Kevin Bacon has played a few big leading parts, and a wealth of secondary roles. He has thus collaborated with an extraordinary number of people in Hollywood. In 1994, three students were trapped in a dorm room at Albright College, Pennsylvania, while a snow storm was raging outside. This is why Craig Fass, Brian Turtle and Mark Ginelli were watching TV when two Kevin Bacon films from the 1980s, *Footloose* and *Quicksilver,* happened to come on one after the other. They started discussing how many films Bacon had actually starred in, and how many people he had worked with. From this idea they built *The Kevin Bacon Game* also known as the *Six Degrees of Kevin Bacon*, of which the object was to link every actor in Hollywood to Kevin Bacon. If, for instance, one wanted to connect British actor Anthony Hopkins to Kevin Bacon, this could be done via Brad Pitt: Hopkins and Pitt collaborated in *Legends of the Fall*, whereas Pitt and Bacon both played in *Sleepers.* This would give Hopkins a so-called *Kevin Bacon Score* of two – being two degrees from Kevin Bacon. The thought of Kevin Bacon being the center of the universe in this way fascinated the three young scholars, and they invented a game where people could just throw random names of actors at them, and then they would make the connections. The trio wrote to Jon Stewart, known to most people today for his satirical *The Daily Show*, but who then had a talk show in his own name. He thought it was a great idea and invited the three people on the show. They also appeared on the most popular morning radio show in the U.S. at the time, *The Howard Stern Show*, and suddenly the whole world knew about Kevin Bacon scores, the *Kevin Bacon Game*, and the theory of six degrees of separation between people. Even Kevin Bacon heard about it and felt insulted at first, until he realized that the game was really a sort of homage to his level of output as an actor. He subsequently wrote the preface to *Six Degrees of Kevin Bacon,* which the three creators published, and he even allowed a board game to be marketed. He has also made fun of himself by referencing the *Kevin Bacon Game* during guest appearances in TV series and TV commercials. The *Kevin Bacon Game* had a great impact on popular culture, and helped put Stanley Milgram's *other* experiment back on the map. But it also got more experienced research capacities thinking.

Hubs

Albert-László Barabási is a Hungarian researcher, born in Romania, who immigrated to America, where he has produced research of revolutionary importance to the way we view Network Society. As early as elementary school, the world around Barabási became aware of his extraordinary mathematical gifts, and at 19 he embarked on a three year course at the University of Bucharest. During those early years he published three articles on Chaos Theory which caught the attention of people around him. In 1991 he moved to the U.S., where he earned his Ph.D. from Boston University three years later. In 1995 he started lecturing and researching at the University of Notre Dame in Indiana. At 32, he became the youngest professor in the history of that prestigious school, and since moved on to Harvard, then to Northeastern University in Boston, where he runs a research center which studies only networks. What Barabási has given the world isn't just the popular and highly readable *Linked,* which discusses the importance of Network Theory in our world, but also his research into the meaning of *hubs.* Hub, like the hub of a wheel. But the word "hub" also means a junction, or a place to go in order to be sent off on one's further journey – such as central stations, airports, etc. A characteristic of such places is that they aren't places one goes to stay for very long. You don't go to an airport to hang out. You go there because it is a junction, and you can move on from there and do other things. And this is precisely where the incredible importance of Barabási's research comes into the picture. He proves the importance of these hubs to networks. But more of that later. First it is important to understand why hubs are intuitively important to Homo Conexus. I have concluded several places in this book that the expansion of the network is something like a raison d'être to Homo Conexus; that Homo Conexus doesn't have a meaningful identity without being part of a network. Hubs make this expansion not only easier but also faster. They are the points in the network that, on the average, comprise more connections than others. But they are not to be mistaken for centers. The difference between a center and a hub is that a center is the *only* junction in a network, whereas a hub can co-exist with other hubs, sharing the common feature that they comprise more connections than the average point in the network. It is obviously desirable to be connected to a hub because its many connections make it possible to expand one's network considerably. This is like a central station, which is more than just a single stop on the way; it's where several railway lines intersect, presenting an array of possibilities for continuing the journey to other destinations.Likewise, hubs among humans are of immense importance. There are many people who enjoy linking up with others, who instinctively gather connections from which they – and others – may benefit. We all know such people. The CEO who has access to a wide and powerful network through the country club or his hunting buddies. The political lobbyist who has connections to decision makers in Congress. The hostess whose social gatherings are always successful because she knows how to connect the right people at the party, and thereby keep conversations going. And then of course Kevin Bacon's omnipresence, which makes him a hub who has worked with practically every actor in Hollywood. In *Linked,* Barabási describes an experiment in which he had an internet search engine canvas all of the internal network of the University of Notre Dame. He wanted to examine the distribution of connections among the many websites the students had made for themselves, or for research findings. There was a rather surprising result. What Barabási studied was how many links any one particular page had – i.e., how many other pages linked to that given page. In this way he sought to demonstrate which pages that were more popular and connected than others. It turned out that 82% (around 270,000 out of 325,000) were connected only to a maximum of three other pages. But 42 pages out of 325,000 were linked to by more than a thousand other pages in the network. So only those 42 pages were popular enough that more than a thousand other pages would link to them. Naturally, there's a sudden rise in popularity and no gradual transition – in other words: The most popular hubs in any network are few.Barabási repeated the experiment among 203 million websites outside the Notre Dame domain, and he found an even more substantial difference in popularity. 90% of the websites were linked to by ten, or fewer than ten, other sites. Only three websites were linked to more than a million. As Barabási puts it:

"These hubs are the strongest argument against the utopian vision of an egalitarian cyberspace. Yes, we all have the right to put anything we wish on the Web. But will anyone notice?"

Barabási thinks that this structure, which he calls *scale-free networks*, is a part of all aspects of life, and shapes the world that Homo Conexus lives in. He further has it:

"In a collective manner, we somehow create hubs, websites to which everyone links. They are very easy to find, no matter where you are on the Web. Compared to these hubs, the rest of the Web is invisible. For all practical purposes, pages linked by only one or two documents do not exist. It is almost impossible to find them."

Transferred to real life, and to networks between people, there's much truth to what Barabási says. According to a survey by headhunter company *Drake Beam Morin*, 64% had found their jobs through the networks of other people. Not job-search websites, but *people networks*. This would not be possible without the existence of hubs. If it weren't for well-connected "hub persons" that wanted to link up the points in the network, then how would the person seeking employment ever find the job, and vice versa, among the masses? Hubs make the points in the network visible to each other – the person who offers a position can find the person looking for a job, etc.

This model offers a different way of looking at hubs:

Text: Used with permission. Martin Rosvall: :
http://www.tp.umu.se/~rosvall

The strength in weakness

Martin Rosvall is a Swedish researcher at the University of Washington. In the model above he has shown how 54 of the 100 most influential people in the world, according to *Time Magazine*, are connected to each other. When the list was published in 2006, Rosvall used Google to find the many connections, and from that he drew this model of networks. It is interesting because it shows a network in which influence and power is distributed between a large number of hubs. The model contains its share of trivial findings, but also many surprises. For instance, it is no surprise that the greatest hub in the network is the President of the United States. As acknowledged "leader of the free world," one has considerable *gravitas*. But it may be more surprising to find that Matt Drudge is another big hub. He is the editor of web based political gossip magazine the *Drudge Report, www.drudgereport.com.* Just like rapper Sean Combs (also known as P. Diddy, formerly Puff Daddy) is a big hub, with more links than Germany's chancellor, Angela Merkel – or even Microsoft founder Bill Gates. Sean Combs is actually only two connections away from George W. Bush, and is so well-connected that he has influence in politics as well as in showbiz. It also portrays a difference in strength in the individual connections, and this is important too. The darker lines are the strongest connections. When there's a distinction between strong and weak connections it is partly due to Mark Granovetter. He is a professor at Stanford University in San Francisco, where he previously headed up the Department of Sociology. As early as the the year 1973 (when Elvis said Aloha from Hawaii) Granovetter introduced a theory of social networks, in his article *The Strength of Weak Ties*. Granovetter had tried to get *American Sociological Review* to publish it in 1969, to no avail. But he managed to get it published in 1973, in a shorter version; in the essay he describes the difference between strong and weak links. The strong connections are our close network, those whom we "ping" the most (*see* Chapter Five), and with whom we consider it most important to keep in touch. The weak connections are either people we're directly connected to, but not very strongly (acquaintances we see once in a while; the local shop owner; a distant cousin). Or it may be those we are linked to via stronger connections. These last ones are particularly interesting. Because this is where it is possible for Homo Conexus to expand the network, which, as previously mentioned, is the driving force behind large parts of Homo Conexus's life. In a 1983 update of *The Strength of Weak Ties,* Granovetter points out that *it is the weaker of the connections that tie the network together*, and thereby create the difference between the isolated individual-centered network of the industrial society and the cohesive, internally-connected network of the Network Society. Granovetter uses the individual "Ego" as an example:

"Ego will have a collection of close friends, most of whom are in touch with one another - a densely knit clump of social structure. Moreover, Ego will have a collection of acquaintances, few of whom know one another. Each of these acquaintances, however, is likely to have close friends in his own right and therefore to be enmeshed in a closely knit clump of social structure, but one different from Ego's. The weak tie between Ego and his acquaintance, therefore, becomes not merely a trivial acquaintance tie but rather a crucial bridge between the two densely knit clumps of close friends."

Granovetter thinks that there probably wouldn't have been any connection at all between the two bodies of friends, if it hadn't been for Ego's random acquaintances. But the weaker connection has further importance:

"It follows, then, that individuals with few weak ties will be deprived of information from distant parts of the social system and will be confined to the provincial news and views of their close friends. This deprivation will not only insulate them from the latest ideas and fashions but may put them in a disadvantaged position in the labor market, where advancement

144

can depend, as I have documented elsewhere (1974), on knowing about appropriate job openings at just the right time."

What Granovetter puts so well here is what drives Homo Conexus: *The expansion of possibilities.* If one sticks to the isolated networks of Industrial Society, it means cutting off the possibilities elsewhere in the network. And the road to these peripheral possibilities is the weak connections. They may be weak but nonetheless extremely important to Homo Conexus. Granovetter mentions the labor market as an example, but fundamentally it's the same in all aspects of life to Homo Conexus. A weak connection to a hub is for instance very valuable, because the hub is the access to other parts of the network, through his, or her, strong and weak connections. And for the same reason it is very important to Homo Conexus to constantly keep the network channels open. Mark Granovetter and Stanley Milgram are among the key players when it comes to research into the networks between people. Barabási and Rosvall are among the leading researchers into how networks behave mathematically, those networks that exist between people. But what about the networks between humans and non-humans? The networks between people, and animals, and things? Can a dog be part of your network? Or how about a physical object – can a table? When I talked to Leonard Kleinrock (see Chapter Three) he said:

"I am absolutely certain that all things and people one day will have an IP number."

The IP address is the number which identifies a computer which is on line. Your broadband modem has an IP address which identifies it on the internet, and your laptop is given an IP address when it accesses your wireless network at home. Your cell phone has an IP address on the telecommunications network if you use the phone for data. But what Kleinrock is saying is that some day little, wireless network chips will enable even plants, dressers and micro-wave ovens to have IP addresses (network-connected micro-wave ovens are already on the market, as a matter of fact). Everything in the world will, according to Kleinrock, be connected in one big internet, and will be able to share information. This may be something of a utopia (or dystopia, depending on your point of view) on Kleinrock's behalf. But thinkers already deal with a similar vision, only without the interference of technology.

Networking with things

French sociologist and philosopher Bruno Latour is one of those people. His actor-network theory is about *everything* being connected in a network, even dead things or non-conscious beings. You're a part of a network of nature, in which physical objects network with you, and you network with them. This may sound like nonsense – how can one network with something which is incapable of communicating – but there is actually a lot of sense to the actor-network theory. Latour believes that it is the connections in themselves which are important. In other words, it is the way that you and the object enter into the network that it is important to focus on. If we look at objects in a room, with a person, the actor-network theory starts to make sense. A person is in a bedroom where he lies down on the bed, while staring at his reflection in one of the mirror doors on the wardrobe. By now the person has already interacted with three other things in the network – the bed, the mirror, the wardrobe. In a Granovetter sense the bed is a strong connection, (because the person laid down on it). The same goes for the mirror (because the person interacts directly with it); while the wardrobe is a weak connection, which the person is connected to only via the mirror. But the mirrors wouldn't have been there in the first place if it hadn't been for the wardrobe, so in this way the weak connection to the wardrobe is important anyway. I wrote that the person in the example had *interacted* with three objects in the network called a bedroom. Some would probably object, because interaction usually means that *both* parties of an interaction are taking conscious action. But the actor-network theory says it's

146

the *function* of the bed which makes the interaction. What the bed contributes to the network is the ability to be laid down upon – softly. It isn't the person that gives the bed softness, but rather the bed which gives softness to the person, when he or she lies down on it. In this way the meeting between the person and the bed enters into a new situation: The person lying down is no longer the same as before he or she laid down, or at least he or she is in a new condition. This new condition has been created by the bed's function and the person's willingness to use this function. The question is whether it's solely the will of the person who uses the bed as a tool to create a new condition, or if the bed itself contributes to the interaction. In the actor-network theory the latter is the case. This all may come off sounding like a homespun philosophy born from too much red wine one late night. But that which comes out of this kind of thinking is highly relevant. It is the *connections* between the things that are the interesting part, not the things in themselves. When one starts to look at the world in this way, the actor-network theory becomes a way of introducing normative notions to Network Society. All of a sudden Network Society becomes a place where one can discuss morals and the philosophies of existence. An interesting example is the old discussion of gun control. Is it right to ban guns because they are dangerous in themselves, or is it – as is the point of those in favor of liberal gun laws in the U.S. – the people that do the killing, not the guns? In the actor-network theory this discussion would be viewed from the connection between gun and human. *It is the connection between the two which creates the problem,* not the weapon or the human separately. From an actor-network theoretical viewpoint, a gun cannot be wrong, neither can a person. But the network connection between the two may easily be wrong – and this can lay the base for a discussion of prohibitive measures. In an interview from 1996 when Mad Cow Disease tore through Europe as a result of feeding cattle food made from crushed bone marrow, Bruno Latour said:

"But people know very well how to act morally or how to be a realist. The questions lie in the connections and controversies surrounding morality, and when you start to pass judgment, you must switch over to objects, conditions and coincidences. Why should grazers not eat bone marrow? Well, now we know why."

In other words, the morals of Homo Conexus are not an absolute standard, according to Bruno Latour, but rather relative to the network connection. There's no use in trying to force ethics like religious dogma on Homo Conexus. Partly because there is always a skeptical alternative within reach, and partly because two networks that are only linked by a weak Granovetter connection, may have fundamentally different moral concepts at two different points in time. With this statement Latour breaks away from some of the most basic philosophical thoughts of the European tradition. The fundamental moral principles are constantly under pressure from the many different situations the ever-changing network subjects the people of the network to. Or more down to earth: Because Homo Conexus incessantly creates network connections to people, animals, and things, it is impossible to maintain moral principles that stand the test of every situation. Instead. Latour has it that moral resources are present in every point in the network, but that the stream of information makes morals more relative to the situation. Morals are being decentralized just like everything else in Network Society. There is no longer a fixed set of moral rules, but the relation between the things in the network are under constant moral evaluation. To take guns as an example again: Can the network relations between a hunter, a rifle and a deer be subject to the same set of moral rules as a gang member, a sawed-off shotgun and a victim? Bruno Latour finds that this is difficult, nearly impossible. Instead he thinks that the individual moral resources in every point in the network, may lend a collective image of the morals of society, albeit in constant flux – precisely as is the case with identities and network connections in the world of Homo Conexus. Latour also suggests that Homo Conexus isn't compatible with the political processes of Industrial

148

Society. He points to the connecting of a person and an object as something that makes the situation different from when the person and the object were separate. Both become something else when they are connected, and therefore we need to think morally about the two as connected and not judge morally on them as separates:

"This is why the discussion between gun control proponents and the others is so interesting, because the left-leaning liberals definition of what human subjects do is just as bad as their opponents'. A human subject becomes something else when it uses the weapon, because it has changed and the weapon has also changed."

As in the example of the softness of the bed, it is impossible to speak of morals unless we look at the specific connections of the network at the specified time. This is also why it doesn't make sense to speak of the economy of free (Chapter Nine), since it is based on a left wing, dogmatic set of values, where it automatically generates social currency to give things away, and where collectivism is the same as social equality. But these dogmas belong to Industrial Society. If one is to find the morals of Homo Conexus, it is necessary to start with the decentralized society, which doesn't have these dogmas. Latour puts it this way, once again speaking of the BSE epidemic of the mid-1990s:

"Should cows stop eating grass, should they go back to only eating grass, should we stop eating cows, should we raise more cattle, etc.? This morality is distributed within the objects themselves, the same way we, in science know how to achieve truth in the classic sense by letting the whole distribution of lab scientists and non-human objects connect. Morality is a path, a way to relate things to each other, so that none of them are treated merely as a means to an end."

Towards the end of the quote, Latour touches upon the moral side of the new solidarity mentioned in Chapter Five. The new solidarity may well be a merchant's solidarity based on the exchange of favors and social content – but there is also an unethical way of exchanging services. There is simply a limit to how much one can use the solidarity to one's own advantage. In Chapter Five I covered how philosopher René Descartes's division of identity into subject and object, became fundamental to the identity formation of people from the Renaissance to this day when the subject is no longer at the center, (another example of decentralization). Latour's actor-network philosophy is on the same page. Descartes's division into subject/object isn't being dissolved, but rather altered and updated. There is still a difference in subjects perceiving objects, but there is a decentralization taking place which equalizes the value of subjects and objects in the formation of an identity or world view. It isn't that Bruno Latour, like Kleinrock, believes that all items will have an IP address in the future, and thereby enough intelligence that we as humans can communicate with them in the network:

"The actor-network theory is not a position that extends subjectivity to objects, and it never has been. Relations are mixed up in many, very complex, philosophical ways between humans and non-humans, and this has been going on since the dawn of man...so it should be apparent that actor network theory is not trying to make the non-human human. It is the study of the ways the two sides have always been integrated."

Latour rather has it, that we have to relate to subjects and objects without preference for one or the other, in order to shape the heterarchic image of the world, which matches Network Society:

"As Whitehead often says, we are not human subjects all the time. We sleep, we engage in routines, and to an extent we are technological forms of reflex actions. Thousands of entities,

*types of entities form our existence temporarily, our subjectivity
cannot be described as being subjective. So what is really
interesting...is placing yourself somewhere other than the
traditional subject-object position."*

So what have we learned about Homo Conexus, and the way
this new type of human enters into society? Well, we have
learned that Homo Conexus has an insatiable need for
decentralization, with the purpose of giving oneself more network
joints with which to network. We have learned that it's a small
world that can be perceived as a big network with a maximum of
six degrees of separation between every person in it. We have
learned that hubs are incredibly important elements in the
network, as Homo Conexus develops his identity, and sees the
possibilities for action that come with an expansion of the
network. We have learned that weak connections are as
important as strong ones, because these are the ones that are
really the path to new self-development. We have noted how
some philosophers see a change these days, in the classical
perception of a person being a subject that experiences the
world as a series of objects and other subjects. And that this
change means breaking away from definitive truths and ethics,
replaced by situational morals dependent on the relations in the
network. A fair share of heavy content. Now, let's get ourselves
into something a little more cheerful and entertaining – Homo
Conexus's use of media.

***

CHAPTER EIGHT:

HOMO CONEXUS AND THE MEDIA

The December, 2006 the cover of the time-honored weekly *TIME Magazine* featured a mirror. It was there to maintain a tradition that was nearly as old as the magazine itself – *TIME's* much anticipated, highly prestigious *Person of the Year*. But in 2006, *TIME* thought that the person of the year was ... the reader holding the magazine! This was unprecedented. But it was also, in a way, to be expected. *Time's* nomination of the ordinary media consumer, the everyday participant in the network society, as *Person of the Year* was somehow the culmination of a year during which the latest development in the media landscape had caused a downright frenzy, bordering on the unreasonable. It was the result of a misunderstanding as old as *TIME Magazine*: That just because something *may* happen, doesn't mean it *will* happen. 2006 was the year that produced the cyber-social phenomenon called Web 2.0. The term emerged from renowned IT-publisher Tim O'Reilly's 2004 conference of the same name. According to O'Reilly, 2.0 was a reference to the optimism surrounding the use of the internet, which had been regained after the "dot.com crash" of 2000/2001. But thereafter, the term 2.0 was to take on a far broader meaning among the general public. Web 2.0 was a design paradigm that gave precedence to simplicity and ease of use, after a period when it had been customary to cram as much as possible into a website's home page. Web 2.0 was characterized by the new, social media which came into play during this time, like MySpace and Facebook in the U.S., BeBo in Great Britain, and Arto in Scandinavia. Web 2.0 was the term used to describe the development that had led to user-generated content – which had become the hottest buzz word of the time. According to this latest trend, the media of the world had now become so democratized that *users had seized power of the web*. Henceforth the old, established media conglomerates would crumble under the pressure of this new user-driven internet, where people were not only media *consumers* but media *contributors*. This is what *TIME Magazine* wrote about the declaration:

"Seriously, who actually sits down after a long day at work and says, I'm not going to watch Lost *tonight. I'm going to turn on my computer and make a movie starring my pet iguana? I'm going to mash up 50 Cent's vocals with Queen's instrumentals? I'm going to blog about my state of mind or the state of the nation or the* steak frites *at the new bistro down the street? Who has that time and that energy and that passion?*

The answer is, you do. And for seizing the reins of the global media, for founding and framing the new digital democracy, for working for nothing and beating the pros at their own game, TIME's Person of the Year for 2006 is you."

TIME also wrote that this declaration might be a little on the romantic side. That's putting it mildly. In fact it was such a romantic dream, so far from truth and reality, that ridicule is almost in order.

"I hate to tell you, but I told you so."

That same year, in 2006, Julie Ralund and I published our book *Generation Network*, as mentioned earlier. It deals with the way young Homo Conexuses use media. In the book we tried to break away from the hysteria, and pull matters further down to earth. We were criticized at the time, but today it is evident that our arguments weren't so far fetched. Granted, the media *have* become democratized. But that doesn't mean that everyone wants to take part in the game.

Network mentality is founded in something else, in more profound social changes, and a shift in the way we perceive the world. It's not about whether you have the time, the need – or even feel like – writing a blog. The 2006 fuss about Web 2.0; blogs; remixing; social media and all that, grew from a superficial assessment of what was going on. To assume that the advent of more democratized media and a more decentralized (once again!) media market was a "revolution," would suggest that it was the media that was changing people... and not the other way around. But the media landscape and the consequent spread of knowledge have always been driven by the progress of man. It was *never* the other way around. Gutenberg didn't just stumble upon a printing press by chance. He invented it because man had come to a point in his development where it was time to decentralize the spread of knowledge, which the church and the state had controlled with an iron fist until then. Similarly, when Paul Baran worked to decentralize tele-communications near the end of the 1950s, to create more stable and safer communication, he did so *because man was ready to become even more communicative.* When Arthur C. Clarke described the theories that have since made satellite communications possible, it wasn't a discovery – it was something man invented, because people wanted to see Elvis say aloha from Hawaii to the entire world. In the same way, it is human progress that has paved the way for Web 2.0 – not vice versa. And this was the big mistake of 2006, and which made *TIME Magazine* look a little foolish when the *Pew Research Center* published its annual report on the condition of the media, *State of the News Media* in 2008. A year and a half after *Time* appointed the common media user *Person of the Year*, the report said this:

"The reality, increasingly, appears more complex. Looking closely, a clear case for democratization is harder to make. Even with so many new sources, more people now consume what old media newsrooms produce, particularly from print, than before. Online, for instance, the top 10 news Web sites, drawing mostly from old brands, are more of an oligarchy, commanding a larger

154

share of audience, than in the legacy media. The verdict on citizen media for now suggests limitations. And research shows blogs and public affairs Web sites attract a smaller audience than expected and are produced by people with even more elite backgrounds than journalists."

The report explains further:

"The prospects for user-created content, once thought possibly central to the next era of journalism, for now appear more limited, even among "citizen" sites and blogs. News people report the most promising parts of citizen input currently are new ideas, sources, comments and to some extent pictures and video. But citizens posting news content has proven less valuable, with too little that is new or verifiable."

If we take a look at developments, there's some truth to that. Only four months after *TIME's* declaration, the technology website Ars Technica said that the growth in blogs was declining again. And when taking a look at the search engine Technorati's list of most popular blogs, the top 20 entries are media that can only barely be called blogs. They are websites with more contributors, almost like an editorial team. Some examples are the political news site *The* Huffington Post, network society media like BoingBoing, and technology media like TechCrunch, Engadget and Gizmodo. Characteristic to all of them is the fact that it is the work of a few people, being read by many. The same goes for Twitter, which has been marketed as a social network, but which, over the course of only two to three years, has become a kind of broadcast medium. It's a medium through which celebrities like Ashton Kutcher, Paris Hilton, and many others can communicate directly, in real time, with their fan base via brief text message bursts.

But once again, it is one way communication, from the few to the many, which is the very definition of an old fashioned "push medium," not a modern, social network medium. The 2010 version of the Pew report mentioned above, acknowledged this development, noting the growth of "citizen journalism" web sites, some of which survive only on startup capital. However, as the report states, new research

"...provides more evidence that even the most established citizen sites are not in a position to take on the job of traditional news outlets. Instead, what has begun to emerge is more of a coming together of the two, particularly at the local level."

So there is a place for citizen journalism on a local level. Just as there always has been with community-based local newspapers, and local radio and TV stations, created by local enthusiasts. This is nothing new. Nor has the need for it apparently grown suddenly in recent years, even if *TIME Magazine* chooses to think so. The whole point of media democratization is to give everybody the chance to be a medium. However, something points to the fact that people just don't feel like it. When *TIME* declared Homo Conexus *Person of the Year* in *2006,* they did so from a perception of distribution. They thought that the power in the media had been distributed so widely that everyone could have a piece of the pie, if they so chose. But that wasn't the case. The invention of the ball point pen didn't make everybody a writer either. The truth is that the power of the media has become *decentralized* (it really is a trend in this book). It's true that the mega-publishers no longer have a monopoly on the spread of news and knowledge. But even though there are more suppliers, more hubs, there is still a large majority of consumers who want to, well, *consume. Not* contribute. As I touched upon earlier, it is a central part of Homo Conexus' identity *to share* – which creates a basis for the viral spread of media. There's no question that the decentralization of the media landscape means that messages can be spread virally among consumers, but it is important to distinguish between user generated content, and *user mediated content.*

You don't lose anything by sharing something that's digital. On the contrary, *sharing creates social currency*, and thereby recognition as being a point in a network that's worthwhile being connected to. Another advantage is that the connections in a network are kept vigorous by sharing. However, it is easy to lose recognition and social currency if one is a creator of content. Shyness didn't evaporate when Industrial Man gave way to Homo Conexus. Being a creator of content also means risking humiliation and mocking, rather than recognition and success. The creator is vulnerable, exposed. This it what drives creative people everywhere: film makers, graphic artists, creative people in advertising. For some, the drive towards creativity or towards recognition is so powerful that the risk of humiliation pales by comparison. Such people have an ability to reach the public, whether via the internet, TV, newspapers, exhibitions, events or any other forum. It was always like that. These are the people who flock to media careers; publish books, record music, make films, write feature articles, become politicians, or in some other way are willing to stick their head up. In Industrial Society, the media were viewed as filters that kept the masses at bay, ensuring that only the worthy got through. Then the internet brought democratization to the media, and everyone suddenly enjoyed the possibility of becoming their own medium, and broadcasting their messages to the world, something else came to light: *The number of people that didn't get through before was actually limited.* And the number of people that had something to say which other people actually wanted to listen to, was even more limited!

A Virus... or mere Diffusion?

There may have come more suppliers of information, and the overall image may have become more varied with the democratization of media. But the number of people supplying information is still minimal compared to the number of people consuming information. As we will see in Chapter Nine, only 1.66% of Wikipedia's users also contribute to the online encyclopedia. Our glimpse at Technorati above also shows that little editorial teams serve tons of readers. Finally there's the prime example of YouTube. It was hailed as the sanctuary of user generated content, because the users could upload their private videos to the world, and if they were interesting enough the masses would spread them, and technically turn zeroes into heroes in this way. But if you look at ViralVideoChart.com where Unrulymedia monitors video traffic on the internet – and where YouTube is predominant, to no particular surprise – then reality shows a different picture. On this day in 2011 , as I am writing this, only one of the most popular videos on Unrulymedia's chart was created by a random user. In fact only 5 out of the top 20 videos on the list weren't created by a professional media business. Most were music videos, movie trailers or TV clips. YouTube and the other video sites that are monitored don't advertise a lot. There really is no other way of discovering the videos on these sites than links from other sites, like search engines, or references from friends. In other words, many people want to convey content to their close network, but only a few generate this kind of content. Once the content has been generated, however, Homo Conexus is crazy about distributing it to friends and acquaintances *because of the need for sharing*. As mentioned before, this paves the way for viral communication, the viral spread of messages. This newer term has been introduced instead of "forest fire effect" or the "word of mouth" spread of knowledge. Partly because word of mouth is so slow. People have always spread knowledge by passing it on to each other. But in the world of Homo Conexus it just takes place a whole lot faster. Not only because Homo Conexus has an insatiable need for sharing (which keeps the network vibrant, and thereby Homo Conexus itself), but because there is now a variety of lightening-fast communications media. Douglas Rushkoff was the first to draw the comparison between the way a virus is spread, and the way a message is spread in the network society. He did so in 1995, in the early years of the internet, when he wrote the book *Media Virus.* It deals with the fact that certain issues which the media find hard to deal with openly, can be spread among the public virally. He says the following about the process:

"I originally used the virus as a metaphor to understand how thoughts and ideas move around. But then I discovered that not only was it a metaphor, but these messages really WERE a kind of virus. Just like viruses they had a protective shell, which made it possible for them to pass through time and space, and they could release very potent ideas which would make people talk about them.

Since then, I wasn't as interested in the viruses themselves, as our cultural immune system which makes us immune towards different viral constructions. Why some things spread and why some don't."

However, Rushkoff points to a *diffusion* in the media as opposed to the viral effect. He says:

"In reality, there's only been two or three really successful viral campaigns in the world. And that's a good thing."

... referring to the marketing industry which took his viral idea and tried to use it as cheap marketing, letting the consumers do the work of the advertising media. The code seems to be: *why not let consumers spread the message and save money on advertising media*? Why not let the consumers tell the world about your brand?

"The problem is that none of these people understand how a virus really works. They just look at the most superficial qualities of individual episodes where there is contagion, and then they create a case study about it without really understanding viral transmission or what it means for the message. They don't understand that society has different types of immune defense systems towards different ideas. The problem is, in a time like this, you have to understand how viruses work if you really want

to change the way people think. You can't just hire any single person to spread your brand virally."

Rushkoff also states that just because something is widely spread, it doesn't mean that it has dug itself in. There's a difference between the spreading of a message, and the effect of viral transmission.

"A lot of what we are seeing is just diffusion and not virality. 200 websites that convey the same message is just the same as 200 copies of a magazine that conveys the same message."

In other words, it is possible to spread a message without getting people to act differently, consume differently or think differently. The latter takes true viral transmission, according to Rushkoff. But what does it take to get to the point where Homo Conexus takes matters into his or her own hands, and starts spreading a message virally? Offhand, it is plain luck, or the "being in the right place at the right time" phenomenon, which come to mind as the answer to that question. But some conditions must be met in order for Homo Conexus to get in gear for real. Convenience is of the essence to Homo Conexus. Naturally this also goes when it comes to media. If it isn't easy, fast and straightforward to share the message, it won't happen. The *instant gratification* induced by sharing cannot be too far away. Authenticity is another factor. If the razor sharp BS-detectors in Homo Conexus are activated, the network person changes swiftly to another channel or medium that seems more credible. In the pursuit of the expansion of the network there's no time to waste on messages that only pretend.

In the same way it is important to give the user some social currency. If that isn't present, then what is it the user is supposed to convey? It must be something tangible which is to be shared, whether it is a physical object, a link to a video or an MP3-file. Or else the communication of sharing makes no sense. Which media live up to this? It may be that the conventional newspapers are experiencing trouble but their following on the web has never been greater – and hence the challenge is to make money from the internet. Nevertheless, it's a fact that web based newspapers are incredibly popular. It's easy to conclude that the newspapers have more users coming in than they have users leaving. Or to put it in another way: The newspapers are now in touch with people they never would have been connected to otherwise (on paper). This is partly due to the big newspapers being very good at making room for people to leave comments, and making it convenient to pass a news story on to others. Through services such as Digg and del.icio.us, through Twitter, Facebook wall posts and "send to a friend" functions, or by showing the web address so that it can be copied and passed on. News is fairly easily transformed into social currency. It is obvious that it is more convenient to use a news site than a conventional newspaper. You don't have to go to the corner shop or the mailbox to get it, you don't have to pay for it, and you don't need to bother discarding it afterwards. It's searchable, it can have video and sound, and yesterday's and last year's news is archived on the page directly. And then there's the *honesty*. No system is likely to be more under pressure of authenticity than the journalistic system. If some content on a news site isn't authentic, then competitors, politicians, user services or the users themselves will see to spread the word about it. Monetizing this, however, is another challenge altogether and a subject that could (and should) fill up a book all by itself. That Homo Conexus would stop watching TV in favor of the internet is also a myth that has been gaining ground in recent years. And it is possible to demonstrate that slightly more time is spent on the internet than in front of the TV. But what most surveys fail to take into consideration is Homo Conexus's built-in need for media multi-tasking. It isn't a question of *either* internet or TV – it's *both at the same time*, as we have previously discussed. The TV isn't getting turned off just because Homo Conexus is online with the laptop while sending text messages to the network. A lot of people believe that the success of Apple's iPad is due to its E-

Reader capabilities. And that the success of the diminutive laptops known as netbooks is due to a low price point. I believe both of them are successful because they are great for browsing the web *while watching television.* TV is also a convenient medium. Everybody has (at least!) one; it's just a matter of turning it on, then you can reach out for the kind of entertainment or stream of information you would like. And if you're wondering if TV has viral potential, just go check out any viral video chart. Everything that isn't music videos, film trailers or user videos is taken from TV. What about radio and free newspapers? Free newspapers are good social currency (they can be taken along and given to others), and convenient media (they're available for pickup most places you travel in the urban landscape and you can throw them away again when you reach your destination) – and although the journalistic level is lower than in the paid-for newspapers, they are subject to the same code of credibility. Radio is incredibly convenient because it is possible to do many other things while listening to the radio, whether it's cleaning, dishes, homework, book keeping or whatever else one has going on. Radio is convenient in relation to multi-tasking, but it is hard to make it very viral – unless it is a web radio station, something which is gaining ground – even on cell phones. So Homo Conexus also listens to the radio. And the reason that most of them still listen to *analog* radio is that it is the most convenient. When web radio becomes just as convenient, it will be time to shut down the analog frequencies.

The most hyped phonebooks in the world

We also have the social networking websites that can also be considered media. Or can they? Is Facebook a medium for broadcasting yourself ... or is it an advanced Inbox that lets you keep in touch with people you already know? Is it an essential part of the function of these social networks, to Homo Conexus, that people they *don't* know can read about them? That seems a given fact in the 2006 hysteria. *The fact that everyone could be seen by everyone else made those media democratized.* But something in the use of social networks suggests that it is less important to get in touch with people one doesn't already know – and that networks are used for rounding up and organizing *contacts one already has*. When we meet someone new it has become as customary to ask if the person is on Facebook, as it was previously customary to ask for his or her phone number. This tendency is reflected in a global decrease in the use of e-mail among the youngest part of the Homo Conexus bunch. As previously mentioned, even back in 2007, Pew Internet published a report on the communicative methods of young people. The paper stated that e-mail was increasingly obsolete in the eyes of the youth. Mary Madden, Senior Research Specialist and co-author of the report, put it this way:

"New technology increases the overall intensity and frequency of their communication with friends, with e-mail being the one glaringly uncool exception in their eyes."

Only 22% of the respondents in Pew Internet's study would admit to using e-mail every day, while 47% sent messages through social network sites on a daily basis. About 54% percent used instant messaging; 60% used text messaging daily; and 70% called friends from their cell phones *every day*. The report also showed that when this study was made, 63% of all American teenagers had a mobile phone. This number has presumably grown considerably since. In most Scandinavian and Asian countries, the number of cell phones is *far greater than the number of inhabitants!*

The life nerve of Homo Conexus is in the pocket

OK, let's just get right down to it:. *The cellphone is by far the most important medium to Homo Conexus.*

It's more than just a communication device; more than just a medium. It is as essential to their survival as clothing; as important to the understanding of the world as eyeglasses are to people with poor eyesight, or hearing aids to the hearing impaired. The mobile phone is the fastest, easiest way to keep your connection to the rest of the network vibrant. This is why there's such a growing social acceptance of sending text messages *even while in the physical company of others* – at least among the under-40 crowd. What's going on is that someone is keeping the rest of his or her network alive – and thereby him- or herself – while maintaining a social network with the people that person is physically with at the time. Usually it isn't necessary to have lengthy conversations, but merely a matter of "pinging" each other, like two computers confirming that they are each on the same network. Young people today often have very short and not very in-depth text message dialogues on their mobile phones:

A: Hey.

B: Hey.

A: What's up?

B: Nada.

A: OK.

B: Cool.

A: Later.

B: Word.

A: Bye.

B: Bye.

American researcher Rich Ling studies the sociology of mobile phone communication for the Norwegian telecommunications giant Telenor. He is also a visiting professor at IT University in Copenhagen. He explains the phenomenon in this way:

"It's called 'phatic communication'. In other words: I'm sending you a message not to coordinate or act, but just to say: I am here!"

Phatic communication is widely spread in the U.S. and in Europe in the form of text messages. But when I met Rich Ling at his office at the IT University in the Orestad of Copenhagen, he told me that in the rest of the world there's another way of undertaking this kind of communication without actual messages.

Namely *missed calls!*

"In the third world they try to keep mobile phone bills down. So instead of calling and having a conversation, you'll let the phone ring twice and then hang up. It's a free signaling system. If you're a plumber, and I would like you to come and fix something for me, I'll send you a missed call, and if you want the job, you can call me back. Or if you are picking me up at the train station, I'll send you a missed call instead of an SMS when I have arrived. This takes place everywhere in Africa, Asia and Eastern Europe."

But phatic communication isn't just about coordination. It is also a social necessity, a way of stretching time, space and social calls. At least according to Mimi Ito, an anthropologist with a Ph.D. from Stanford University, who now teaches and researches at UCLA in young people's use of media in the U.S. and Japan. She is mostly preoccupied with what goes on in between peoples' *"flesh meets"* – meeting physically. Ito explains that young people today prolong the physical meets using the cell phone, for instance for warming up prior to a date using text messaging. This dialog can be about how much they're looking forward to seeing each other; the clothes they're thinking about wearing; coordinating the time; whether there are any changes to the plan, etc. After the date the *communication continues* with follow-ups: "Had such a great time yesterday," "It was really nice what you said about my eyes," or even "I just saw the shoes you were talking about on sale at so-and-so's." Ito calls this *tele-nesting*, the building of nests from a distance. The "nest" consists of the common currency the two text messaging love birds are accumulating through their communications. Even though the physical meeting may have been brief, it is expanded mentally in time and space. This is backed by a 2008 Pew Internet study which found that a majority of young people don't even consider text messaging "writing." To them it's a "conversation" – and the act of sitting down to write something is an entirely different process. French sociologist Christian Licoppe calls the phenomenon *connected presence*, a new kind of midway point between physical absence and physical presence. Licoppe believes that the many kinds of telecommunications that Homo Conexus indulges in to keep dialog constant, are breaking down the border between physical and non-physical presence. Homo Conexus is in a constant dialog with the network, because without these connections there is no identity – and therefore no existence.

Conexo, ergo sum: I link, therefore I am. Remember?

Licoppe thinks that Homo Conexus has developed

"... a 'connected' management of relationships, in which the (physically) absent party gains presence through the multiplication of mediated communication gestures on both sides, up to the point where copresent interactions and mediated distant exchanges seem woven into a single, seamless web."

Translated into words for mere mortals, it means that communication across distances, and physical company, can be intertwined in a way that makes it hard to separate the two. Perhaps you've already experienced this yourself: "Did that talk over recipes take place on IM or Facebook? Was it something we discussed on the phone? Or the last time we were together?" "When was the last time I saw Jason? – hey, it's coming up on a full year. But we've been writing each other on iChat everyday, so I haven't felt out of touch with him." Rich Ling was so kind as to elaborate on Licoppe's thinking for me:

"'Connected presence' is the idea of a continuous conversation that takes place throughout your day. Not necessarily face to face, but maybe you meet with a friend over coffee in the morning, and later you'll send him a message that 'The shoes you were talking about are on sale in this or that store." It's all about a daily, long conversation."

According to Ling, the cell phone has become the "glue" that ties us together socially, because of its function as the connecting point in the Brave New Network our world consists of.

"Mobile phones build social coherence in a way that no other information or communication technology can do. Some come close, such as the PC with IM, chat and e-mail. But if you're online when your wife is trying to have a conversation with you, you tear the social coherence apart. The mobile phone is not quite as isolating and can cultivate coherence, even over great distances."

This socialization in the middle of the deconstruction of time and space is typical to Homo Conexus. One of the cultural changes that Homo Conexus has brought along is a more relaxed attitude towards appointments with close relations. Instead of agreeing upon a place and time, and jotting it down in a calendar like the old days, it isn't unusual for Homo Conexus to wait until well into the very day of the appointment, to find out when and where the appointment is taking place. And it's socially acceptable to change or adjust the plans *via* text messages. This is what Rich Ling calls *micro-coordination*. His example: We used to pick a place and a time. But now, after the emergence of cell phones, we micro-coordinate all the time. A micro-coordination conversation could sound like this, to quote Rich Ling:

"Where are you?"

"I'm over here."

"Okay, but it's better over here"

"But there's a café here."

"Okay, I'll come over there, then."

This little peculiar negotiation is making the old time-based system obsolete.

But Rich Ling thinks that micro co-ordination and the function of the mobile phone as network "glue" works only in tight social circles:

"There's a limit. We still use time measurement. We still say "I'll be there in ten minutes" or "I can be there 10:30". If you are talking about three to four people, micro-coordination works. But I can't call the airline and say "Hey, I'm late, could you hold the plane for me?" It doesn't work in large systems. But in small social groups it works very well."

This goes well with the limitations to the ultimate freedom in the work place, which we touched upon in Chapter Six. Rich Ling does say that the reason micro co-ordination works in close circles is that the cell-phone is the glue of little networks, such as close friends and family:

"The mobile phone is an instrument for the intimate group, the close family and your friends. A group that sticks together and keeps in touch."

You have only 150 friends. Deal with it.

Mark Granovetter's idea of strong and weak connections also applies to mobile phone communication. You may have 600 phone numbers in your cell phone, and 600 friends on your Live Messenger buddy list. But if you take a look at who you've actually called, or been in touch with recently, it may quickly be evident that there are perhaps 10-15 close connections, and around 150 weak connections, which it is possible to really relate to. That isn't just a random figure I yanked out of the air. 150 is the so-called Dunbar Number, named after Oxford University anthropologist Robin Dunbar. In 1993 his research results showed that the part of the human brain used for conscious thinking, the neocortex, can relate to only 150 steady, human connections at a time. He arrived at this conclusion by studying the abilities of primates, and then multiplying the number to fit the size of the human brain. However, Dunbar believes that social networks like Facebook may *in principle* train the human to be able to contain more connections. But there's still a long way to go before we reach the 5,000-person limit to how many friends one may have on Facebook. An analysis published in *The Economist* in February of 2009 seems to confirm this fact. The magazine had asked Facebook's own Cameron Marlow, a sociologist, to come up with some numbers. Dr. Marlow found that the average number of friends on Facebook is 120, which isn't far from the Dunbar Number of 150. However, the article also notes that there are always a few people who create spikes in the average number, having over 500 friends. Those Facebook users with more than 500 friends are typically hubs – people who are good networkers, and who attract Facebook friends who wish to broaden their networking possibilities. But the interesting part of the study is how many people actually have *active* relationships within social networks. These are the ones whose status one comments on, or with whom one communicates via the internal messaging system in Facebook. For the average user, with around 120 Facebook friends, this amounts to only 7 such connections for men, 10 for women. So most people on Facebook communicate actively with only a small number of other people. And the number of people the hubs communicate with, actively, is only a fraction of the people that he or she is connected to. For those people with more than 500 friends, the men have steady communication with 17 others, and the women with 26. This seems to confirm Mark Granovetter's idea of strong and weak connections. Even the most well-connected hubs have strong connections to a number of people in a tight little network; weak connections to many more. Give it a thought the next time you clean out the phone book in your cell phone. And should you grow disenchanted on the way, then don't ditch the mobile phone. Rich Ling's next book deals with the mobile phones having become a *social fact* – in line with Emile Durkheim's definitions. Durkheim believes that there are things in society which must be taken for granted in order for everything to be joined together. One example is our language. Money might be another. The question is whether Homo Conexus has brought us to a point where the cell phone has become a genuine social essential. Rich Ling thinks so:

"In my next book I am going to work with what I call "taken-for-granted-ness". That there are things in society and life that we take completely for granted. Durkheim called these social facts – something that is part of society before you are. Something you have to accept in order to become a legitimate part of the community. Something society needs in order to even exist. Money is an example. If you decide you want to try to get by without money in society, it can be done. But it's going to be hard, and your relationship with the rest of society will be awkward. My theory is that the mobile phone is becoming one of these social facts."

Seen in this light, it isn't so strange that the cell phone is as important to Homo Conexus as the very air he or she breathes. Not only is it the main way to maintain a network and thereby one's identity. It is also a demand from the society surrounding Homo Conexus.

CHAPTER NINE:

HOMO CONEXUS CONSUMES -

THE ILLUSION OF FREE

The sign was hanging above the store for everyone to see. The pink logo on the white background was unmistakable – the presence of the Swedish telecommunications company Telia had been inevitable for years. But this sign was different. It was an advertisement for *the illusion of free*. In the beginning of 2009, Telia started running a campaign which offered customers a free movie ticket for a friend every Tuesday – that is, if they had a Telia subscription. In other words: If your cell phone says Telia, you can be the big spender every Tuesday and treat your BFF to a movie. Just pay your own ticket, and Telia will throw another one your way. And this isn't just a limited time "one-off." It's something that is always part of being with Telia. Of course it is always fantastic to get something for free. The truth is that it isn't really free at all – it just appears that way.

It's the *illusion* of free.

But this "illusion of free" is also incredibly important. It is part of the very foundation of the network society, and an element essential to the new way of consuming epitomized by Homo Conexus. Because when you get something for free, there's no payment process and you get *instant gratification*. It's *convenient*.

There are no barriers between you and what it is you want. And for someone who's used to getting information and entertainment for free at the click of the mouse or pressing a touch screen, this removal of barriers is crucial. In fact, it's even more important than old sales arguments such as price and quality. There seems to be a general consensus that people, especially young people, have become used to getting something for nothing. Music is something you download for free from the internet. The same goes for films. You can play online games for free using the internet, and news is also something you no longer pay for. The major newspapers are particularly worried about that last fact, and there's an ongoing debate whether it is even possible to make people pay for digital content or other services of the network society. And yet, after a period of giving away content for free, many media outlets are now charging for content again, putting up "pay walls" which stops the user in his tracks, interrupts his flow and keeps him from *instant gratification*. Some of these initiatives will work for people who are used to going through arduous processes to pay for stuff. Well, Homo Conexus isn't. Maybe that's why The Times of London went from 21 million online readers a month to merely 2.7 million when they introduced a paywall. And only a mere 105.000 people out of those 2.7 million chose to subscribe by the fall of 2010, approximately 30.000 of which were iPad or Kindle subscribers. It's a staggeringly low number for such a huge media outlet. That's not to say that people aren't interested in paying, they're just not interested in being interrupted in their search for instant gratification. It isn't about whether or not you pay, but it's about *paying in a new way*. As we shall see, Homo Conexus is willing to pay a reasonable price for services – it just has to happen in a way that appears to be free. *The illusion of free.* In recent years, there's been much discussion about whether the network society is also a society where everything is free. Chris Anderson of *Wired* magazine followed up his hugely successful book about *The Long Tail* with a book about *Free*. Unfortunately, the world changed once again as he was writing it, and the allure of an economy based on free turned out to be a mirage. Also, before the book came out, the app revolution happened. It all of a sudden became insanely easy to download new software to your smartphone – initially the iPhone – so a lot of people did it. But what was really interesting was the fact that it was just as easy and convenient to *pay* for the applications as it was to download them. And that made the whole difference. It's structured impulse-buying. Instant gratification with a price tag. Anderson didn't retract his words. Instead, he ran a story in the August 2010 issue of Wired, which carried the words *The Web Is Dead* on its cover. Why did Anderson do a 180? Because of the popularity of paid-for apps for the cell phone and other platforms, where a new economy is currently building up. It's not about the money; it's about the payment process. There are still a lot of people talking about how we should take money out of the equation in the network society. It's a discussion that's been going on for more than 25 years. However, this book claims that the advocates of free are mistaken. And to best explain why that is the case, here is a run-through of the thinking behind the economy of free.

The Ideology of Free

After the breakthrough of the internet in the Western world in the mid-1990s, some thinkers began speaking of a return to the gift economy. In that system, the exchange of gifts, and the relationships established by the act of giving, were the cornerstones of the network society. It's easy to see what might have prompted that thinking: Many paid services were all of a sudden made redundant by the internet. Many things became completely free, like finding a phone number or acquiring new music. Classic literary works could be downloaded for free, and pictures of pop stars and actors that were previously findable only as 8x10-inch promotional glossies or in fan magazines, now floated freely in cyberspace.But it was the open source wave of the 1990s in particular which got the thinkers thinking. It was now possible to get free computer tools and software products, which other companies would charge substantial money for. Having an e-mail address became free of charge, and because you could check your e-mail via a webpage, buying an e-mail client wasn't necessary. It wasn't necessary to buy an office package from one of the giants like Microsoft – others had developed alternatives that were free and practically as good, with word processing, spreadsheets, and whatever else you needed. In fact you didn't even need Windows any longer. You could save cash by downloading an open source operating system based on Linux and use that instead. Completely free, easy, simple. This made a number of thinkers draw comparisons to the exchange of services and goods which took place *before* money found its place in the world. Prior to money becoming the intermediary for services and products, people would *trade* services and products with one another. And this was often done for semi-altruistic reasons –without expecting anything in return. A more recent example of this was the establishment of the GNU project in September of 1983. At that time, the home computer was on its way to becoming a household item, while computers in universities and other big institutions were largely run by the operating system UNIX. But UNIX cost money, and to some people this was seen as a hindrance to allowing the masses access to powerful computing. The project grew from this persuasion – that software and the use of a computer shouldn't be dependent on social status or income, but should be a form of human right. The man behind the GNU project, Richard Stallman, wanted to create a free alternative to the paid-for operating system UNIX. The apt, self-referencing abbreviation GNU stands for "GNU's Not UNIX!" This altruistic attitude of Stallman's had its roots in his left wing persuasion. He emphasized the moral and value-based reasons for the creation of GNU when the program was launched:

"Software sellers want to divide the users and conquer them, making each user agree not to share with others. I refuse to break solidarity with other users in this way."

So, Stallman's motive for starting GNU was a showdown with what he saw as a capitalistic strangulation of the consumer. If GNU wasn't decidedly a socialist revolution in the Reagan Era in the U.S., it was at least something that seemed like it. Stallman dedicated his life to the development and distribution of free software. To bring a structure to the way software was being spread, Stallman developed licenses that worked as rules for copying and creating free software. The *GNU General Public License* was introduced by Stallman in 1989, and was a set of rules that instructed the user to generate openness about the software. It was essential, for instance, that a person offering software under the GPL license wasn't allowed to technically hinder the spread of the software. But the most important element in the GPL license was that the source code had to be open. GPL-licensed software code should always be open to any other person with the purpose of further developing and spreading the product. This gave name to the phenomenon of *open source* software. Another proponent of this movement is law professor Lawrence Lessig. In the first decade of the new millennium he became very popular for establishing *Creative Commons*, a collection of different licenses which could serve as an alternative to the somewhat rigid and old-fashioned copyright laws of his country, the U.S.A. (European copyright laws aren't quite as rigid, which is why Creative Commons hasn't caught on there quite as much yet). Creative Commons, heavily inspired by GNU, lets you decide who is allowed to copy your work and who isn't. It lets you determine if it's OK to make money from your product, and finally, whether you need to be credited when work passes through your system. Lessig became the poster boy of the free software movement, and is one of those who see the network society as a rebirth of the gift economy. According to him, this happens by making cultural products such as music and film more freely available in order to create a new, more liberated, creative, cultural paradigm. But back to the free software. When you download the *Firefox* browser, it's because a community of open source developers and programmers have come together to build a product everyone can benefit from. It's actually a descendant of the *Netscape Navigator* browser, which was the first real browser to gain mass popularity on the World Wide Web back in the mid-nineties. As previously mentioned, there are all kinds of free software out there, built under these conditions. You can get a free alternative to Windows in the

Ubuntu version of *Linux*. You don't have to buy an office suite – Sun's *OpenOffice* is free. Open Source internet browsers and e-mail clients are yours to have without any payment. And then we haven't even begun to mention the thousands of free services on the internet that are extremely useful, and who are *not* open source. Like Snooth.com, a combined gathering place, market and resource for wine enthusiasts, as well as for Mindmeister.com where it is possible to organize one's work in "mindmaps," completely free of charge. Or Hulu.com where American television fans can watch the latest episodes of their favorite TV shows for free (or pay to watch old ones). Everything is free all of a sudden. Or so it seems. In his *Free* book, Chris Anderson argues for the gift economy as one of the many types of "free concepts" that permeates the Network Society: *People give things away to achieve non-commercial advantages.* However, most people agree that the prestige or the expectation of a certain degree of popularity or influence – or even the relations one could establish by offering services for free or giving things away – is a powerful motivating factor in itself. According to the thinkers behind the "free ideology", giving things away, or making appealing things available, could increase a person's value within the network, and make a person attractive.

Social Capital, not social currency

This is not new at all. It's a way of achieving what the renowned French sociologist Pierre Bourdieu called *social capital*, meaning "the resources at one's service as a result of one's ability to network."According to Bourdieu, social capital can be exchanged for monetary currency in varying ways. Generally, Bourdieu claims that a strong network can be converted into financial gain, if only one is skilled enough. It appears to be relatively simple. We all recognize the businessman whose network has placed him in the upper bracket of society, or how one may find a better paid job through one's network. But the aspect of Bourdieu's work relevant here, is the thought that something which is free easily can provide a healthy bottom line, and do some good for society at the same time. Chris Anderson and the other advocates of the gift economy are convinced that "freeconomy," as these thinkers also call it, is the fundamental economic factor in the network society because *it helps the benefactor earn social capital.* Which, by the way, shouldn't be confused with the concept of social currency that was discussed in chapter five. In other words, if you give something away for seemingly altruistic reasons, you get respect and recognition – but you also get attention and popularity. This builds relations between people, and connects the dots of the network. According to this theory, it is the gifts which connect the points in the network society, and allow Homo Conexus to more easily form relationships with others. The Australian analyst Kylie Veale, who holds a Ph.D. in Internet Studies, concluded this in an article as early as 2003:

"The Internet today is a mix of 'the free and the fee', though it still remains in part a gift economy."

And if that goes for the internet, it goes for humans, too – which is one of the premises of this book, right?For companies it can often be profitable to give things away just to acquire a certain image. Many IT journalists are trying to tell stories of how Google has become a giant corporation the size of Microsoft and therefore should be treated with the same degree of skepticism. But the popularity and identity of Google is still linked with change, revolution from the roots up, and not least, *free gifts in the form of one clever service after another.* That is why Google's social currency is such a giant resource. But I claim that it isn't the "save-a-buck" element of the gift giving which had brought Google so much social currency. Google gives away internet tools (financed by advertisements) in the hope of letting the individual user evolve and be productive. This is a kind of productivity which the thinkers Lessig, Anderson and Stallman believe should be reciprocal. In order for the gift economy to work, whatever is being produced using these "gifts," should also be returned in the form of gifts. *Sharing is a central part of the network society*, as we discussed in Chapter Five. The believers in the gift economy often cling to a concept they call "the circle of giving." It is inspired by the poet Lewis Hyde, who has inspired nearly everyone who seriously discusses gift economy today, in his book *The Gift*, in which he writes:

"...when gifts circulate within a group, their commerce leaves a series of interconnected relationships in its wake, and a kind of decentralized cohesiveness emerges."

This sounds exactly like Homo Conexus: Decentralization, power of cohesion, and internal relations. Right?

Except it also sounds like Karl Marx.

Like it or not, there's a political slant to the free software movement. The new wave of gift economy thinking started as a left wing project of Richard Stallman, and more than 20 years later it still bears the same Marxist resemblance coming from Lawrence Lessig as well as Chris Anderson.

As Christian Fuchs puts it in his book *Internet and Society: Social Theory in the Information Age:*

"Lawrence Lessig employs the term free culture *for the idea that technology "could enable a whole generation to create... and then through the infrastructure of the Internet, share that creativity with others."*

Marx perceived freedom as a gift economy, a world of freedom characterized by cultivated individuality, collective activities, plenty, bringing down the level of hard work through technological innovation, the letting go of the principle of performance, free production and the distribution of goods... Based on this concept of freedom, free culture not only means that digital knowledge can be used freely, but that *no exchange of money is taking place* – things are free. The exchange economy replaced by the gift economy. A free culture based on a wide concept of freedom. It is a non-capitalistic culture. Marx, extreme leftism and communism lurk in the shadows, with many of the believers in the gift economy who think that the relations and social currency of the network society is created by "free-ness." It is no wonder that one of the names the anti-copyright movement goes by is the copy-*left* movement. It's not just wordplay. Thankfully, most of the movement, which tries to discuss e.g. old copyright thoughts in the context of the new age, is pretty serious and moderate about it. But minority factions within the group have also seen it as means of leveraging an extreme left wing agenda which would even go so far as ending copyright. You can even find people with these views in Silicon Valley, which bases a lot its revenue on intellectual property. Copyright is essentially a form of property rights and is considered a Human Right by the UN. Ending property rights does sound a little like North Korea…right?

Where Logic Ends

To be fair, I will say that none of the examples Chris Anderson uses are as utopian as Stallman and Lessig might wish. He rather imagines the gift economy as integral to our existing economy, and not a complete replacement. This is a pattern which occurs time and time again in the transition to the network society: Rather than a complete revolt, it is *a gradual impact* that nonetheless has great consequences. In the article in Wired which later became the basis for the book, he uses the following realistic example of the gift-economy integrated in the present:

"Low-cost digital distribution will make the summer blockbuster free. Theaters will make their money from concessions — and by selling the premium moviegoing experience at a high price."

Chris Anderson has already been proven partially right, as demonstrated by the Telia example at the beginning of this chapter. It is Telia that pays to let its customer be able to take a friend to the movies – all to compete with major Scandinavian telco TDC's giving away free music to its customers. Just like the US telco Cricket has recently started doing. Both Anderson's theoretical idea, and the real-life Telia campaign show how Homo Conexus is being catered to by the introduction of free gifts along with paid-for services. And this is where I claim that the logic ends. First of all there isn't – in the real world – anything at all, which is truly free to the consumer. Second, the utopian gift economy idea is hardly feasible should it be introduced to the real world. Third, and most importantly, it isn't the price that has made the free services popular with Homo Conexus. It is the availability, the *convenience* of these products. To take the first point first: Nothing which is perceived as free in the realm of the gift economists is *really* free. Take Chris Anderson's cinema example. The cinemas aren't about to let their business tank.They will just mark up prices on popcorn and candy, and as Anderson himself explains, charge more for special events like premieres, etc. In the Telia example, there's no doubt who pays the bill. Telia's marketing budget is covering that extra seat for your buddy. And in the end you pay, because Telia's books would be a sorry sight if they spent more money on marketing than they had money coming in from customers. If Telia's strategy succeeds, the concept will give the company more customers, and that is the additional profit that pays for the show. It seems free, but it isn't. The free, on-demand music offering that Scandinavian telcos are currently giving away to their customers costs a huge lump sum in compensations for rights owners, record companies, musicians and songwriters. But to the telcos it is strictly marketing – a service that is free of charge to loyal customers. But it isn't free. You can't use the service without being a broadband or mobile broadband customer – and hopefully no one is naïve enough to think that the telcos would lose money for the customers' sake. They don't deal in altruism. And although those free initiatives are guaranteed to bring more customers – and thereby a bigger turnover – there are still costs connected to sending this music to people. Just the maintenance of the technical facilities (copper or fiber optic lines, servers, etc.) it takes for customers to use the

180

system costs a fortune. In the end the customer pays. But what about Wikipedia, then? This online, user-driven encyclopedia that has all the information in the world, including some of the information included in this book? In 2007, Chris Anderson used Wikipedia as an example of the gift economy when speaking at a conference. He emphasized it as a place to gain social capital by contributing to the community, right along the lines of Bourdieu's thinking.

The leeches of Wikipedia

But if it is true that the gift economy demands reciprocal behavior – giving something back – then Wikipedia is actually one of the worst examples. Because Wikipedia is really one of the best examples of what is called *leeching* in the piracy world, meaning hogging content without contributing. During the writing of this book, I took a quick glance at Wikipedia's own statistics page, and it revealed that the English version of Wikipedia has around 3.5 million contributions, created by 13,845,482 registered users of which only 136,946 had contributed anything in the past month (January 2011). In other words there were 136,946 contributors per month – or 0.9% of all the people that were registered and could theoretically help edit the Wikipedia articles. But that's nothing when you compare how many people actually contribute, to how many people simply use the service. The research company ComScore estimates that close to 190 million users visits the English version of Wikipedia every month. In other words, only 0.07% of the Wikipedia users contributed anything during the month of August 2010. The rest merely *received* the gifts. And yes, some of the contributors will probably gain social currency – there certainly isn't any other kind of payment involved – but it takes some research to find out who wrote exactly what. Remember the last time you looked something up on Wikipedia, and looked for the author? But isn't Wikipedia cheap to run? It's just a few servers and some ultra-simple web design, right? Wouldn't take much to keep it going, would it? On the contrary.

During 2010 Wikipedia did a donation drive online, and reached its goal of collecting $16 million in private donations to keep the company afloat through a time still impacted by the recession of 2008-9. Wikipedia doesn't carry advertisements, so the only real income for the running and development of the company is from private donations - which is now an ongoing thing. But people were happy to be able to help with that. During the last fund raising period, Wikipedia showed some of the comments made by people who were donating – often small sums – to the cause. All were happy remarks from people who appreciated having access to free information about nearly anything. Their comments could be seen on the homepage of the foundation behind Wikipedia, The Wikimedia Foundation. Looking through the comments there are only few references to the "free movement"; as well as lots of affectionate declarations. A woman named Sonja Rose made this comment along with her donation: "Wiki helps expand my world." Farrukh Salim wrote simply, "Good job." Moreover, everyone seems to be crazy about the efficiency Wikipedia works with, and the fact that Wikipedia makes knowledge accessible to everyone. But practically nowhere does anyone mention that they love Wikipedia *because it lets them save money.* On the contrary, all the people who donated money just paid to use the service – by securing its immediate future. There's no doubt that there is a collective, idealistic idea of distributing information democratically via many donations. But the majority express the simple joy of *using* the site, and would therefore gladly pay for its continued existence. The number of users compared to the number of registered wikipedians above, does point in the same direction. So, what is really going on, when so many people donate money in order for Wikipedia to continue? Is it an example of gift economy? Hardly, since the presence of money works against that possibility. No, it's more like the time when the rock band Radiohead released their album *In Rainbows* in 2007. In the same way, the album could be downloaded from the band's home page, while users could just pay whatever they thought was a fair price. It turns out that a considerable audience ended up paying *what the album would have cost in an online store*, and that the average price was around £4 or, expressed in U.S. terms, about $6. That's less than the normal retail price, but more than four times more than the band would have made through an ordinary release of a CD. Certain reports, including those of Gigwise.com (reports which the band has called "exaggerated"), claimed that the album was downloaded 1.2 million times on the internet. In 2007, a spokesman for the band said:

"Most people are deciding on a normal retail price with very few trying to buy it for a penny."

The price itself is, even in times of financial crisis and high unemployment, not the primary factor when Homo Conexus enters into new methods of distribution. It isn't because Wikipedia is free that people are happy with it. There are two other reasons. One reason is convenience, which we will deal with in the next chapter. The other is *the illusion of free.*

The Illusion Of Free

I mentioned *the illusion of free* at the beginning of this chapter, but as a term it is difficult to understand if one doesn't know of the mindset behind the wave of free services, and of the gift-economy. So, that's why we had to take the long way around to arrive at this point. The thoughts behind the wave of free services and the gift economy are all very well in themselves, but they miss one central point: *Why* is it so interesting to Homo Conexus to get free stuff?
As we can see from the Wikipedia example, social currency isn't always gained by giving things away in the network society. Wikipedia is also a good example that many people are still willing to pay for something they are happy with – *even* if they come from a culture of sharing. I dare say that the secret lies in the fact that Wikipedia isn't really free... it just appears to be. When you look something up on Wikipedia you first of all expect a Google-like convenience and fast response. If Wikipedia had a

graphically heavy interface, which took forever to load, it wouldn't be the big player in the network society that it is today. But you also expect that the seeking of information is free of charge. It is "free" – but it isn't. To even get as far as being able to use free information services like Wikipedia, you must first have a computer. How many times can you take a cab down to the local library for the amount of money a computer costs? You also need a broadband connection, and even though they are not as pricey as they used to be, it all adds up. The electricity that powers your venture in cyberspace also comes at a price. And finally you may be one of those who are willing to make a contribution to Wikipedia, when they ask for it. The fact is, you can't use free services or software on the internet without hardware. And the hardware isn't worth much without either free or paid-for software. And you wouldn't have used the electricity you use to run your computer if you hadn't used this software. Without the software your computer would make a very expensive door-stop. Or to put it differently: Even if you only use free services of free software on the internet, then you paid for the service you get all in all, anyway. The price you paid for the computer is really the price you've paid to use free software. Even if you're irresponsible enough to get your music, films and TV illegally on the internet via Bittorrent or one of the other illegal clients, you still pay. Because, what *else* would you use your broadband connection for? Other free services? And apart from the money you've paid for a door-stop which the free services and software turn into something useful, you also pay with your attention and time. As soon as you put yourself in a position where you're being marketed to, you put yourself in the position of possibly making a purchase, which may result in your paying an additional cost for some product, because the power of advertising works! You don't feel that you pay when you use Google either. But you do – Google is financed by advertisements, and *you sell your attention*. Have you noticed that Google scans the content of your recently sent e-mail, so that when the recipient reads it, Google advertises products that are related to what you wrote? The waiving of your right to privacy is the price for "free" services. And add to that the share of your PC, power and internet budgets which are connected to your use of Google. No matter if it is commercials on the internet or on TV, then you risk your money, time and attention when you're willing to receive "free" entertainment and news, paid for by advertisements. Remember, those advertisers pay a lot of money to get to you. So you are in their sights constantly whenever you indulge in content financed by advertisements. Oh yeah, TV – do you have cable? Or satellite? Not free either, is it? You need to dish out a decent lump sum every month just to be able to expose yourself to commercials. In the UK, the BBC charges a TV license fee from almost all UK citizens that is paid once a year and then forgotten about. Not exactly free either – but on an everyday basis it feels like it. What Homo Conexus really wants isn't free stuff but *the illusion of free.* It must *feel* free. It must an *instant gratification* with no payment process to slow down the experience. When the Brits pay the fee to the BBC they don't think about it in the time in between. During that time watching TV is just free. Water costs so little, and is paid for so rarely, that the faucet seems like a free service. But it's not. And if you think the water in the faucets in the public park is free, then look at your tax statement once again. Homo Conexus has come into the world after a bill is no longer something that turns up in the mailbox, but is paid automatically through direct debit.Homo Conexus is used to having hundreds of channels to choose from on the TV, in return for a little sum that's being paid every month, also automatically. Homo Conexus is used to the internet supplying all kinds of "free" things all the time. If you need information, you need to pay for it only if you can't find it on the internet. Communication must feel free too, which is one of the reasons that text messages became so popular with Homo Conexus – you didn't need to worry about sending them off. The text message example can be compared to micro-payments – that little payments are being made all the time, and therefore don't make a big impact on the budget. But there are also many examples of *that* not working. If it were the size of the fee that was pivotal, then why would teenagers at the turn of the millennium gladly pay $4 for a ring tone, while they wouldn't pay $1 for a song at a legal MP3 store? Because the convenient availability of the ring tone was fundamental. When you sent a text message ordering a ring tone, you don't feel like you pay. As mentioned before, the music futurist Gerd Leonhard has compared the future need for music with that of faucets: You just need to be able to turn the music on, and think no-more of it. That's the reason the illegal music services have always beaten the legal paid-for services. *You just had to turn the handle and let the music run.* The music industry was the first to take a serious hit from the new consumer habits. But after stumbling along for much of a decade, they got it right. They understood that convenience is more important than price, and that the real reason for all the piracy was all about instant gratification. For anyone who is having trouble marketing and selling products to Homo Conexus, there's a very valuable lesson in what happened to the music industry. The film industry is going through the same motions now, and books may be next. So maybe it would be a good idea to take a closer look at what happened when people stopped paying for music.

When Music Became "Free"

Everyone thought Radiohead were pioneers in 2007, when they released *In Rainbows* and asked people to pay whatever they wanted. But it really wasn't that innovative. In 1973, when Elvis said *Aloha From Hawaii,* there were different ways of paying for his service. Some TV stations were kind enough to pay for the rights on behalf of their viewers, so they could listen to Elvis for free (well *almost free*, and this is important, as we will later see). Other TV stations across the world who broadcast the concert, demanded money from their viewers, and later fans could pay for the vinyl record which was released in connection with the concert. The concert tickets also cost money, but there was no set price. Elvis simply asked people to pay what they could, and the proceeds went to a Hawaiian cancer research foundation. This is the same method the band Radiohead would be called revolutionary for using, when they released *In Rainbows* – only without the charity aspect.But despite the charity angle, money was in fact exchanged in different ways when Elvis took the stage on January 14, 1973. In 1999 it became possible to become part of the experience – for free. Or almost. But first we need to go back another five years to understand one of the great events that separates the industrial society from the network society.

What was that event?

In 1994, research in the area of compressing both sound and image had been going on for quite some time. The CD had already introduced the public to digitally reproduced music, and laser discs had facilitated the home viewing of films with heretofore unheard-of high quality. The analog satellite transmission which Elvis used in January of 1973 was being replaced by digital signals. But when sound and images are transformed into digital ones and zeroes, it usually takes up a lot of data capacity. Therefore it made sense to compress the size of these lumps of data, when they were to be distributed through the air in the form of digital radio (which we know today as satellite radio in U.S. and DAB in Europe), or via satellite. For some time, acoustic scientists had been attempting to manipulate sound and images in labs all over the world. Sound data was removed which the ear couldn't hear anyway, and image data which the eye couldn't process was dropped from video sequences. This minimized the size of video and sound files, and films could now be contained on the little DVDs instead of on laser discs, and radio could be streamed via the internet, which was gaining ground in the Western world. One of the means of compression which quickly became popular came from the Frauenhofer labs in Germany. Frauenhofer is really a collection of 58 institutes financed by both public and private funds. It was from Frauenhofer that the program *L3enc* was put on the internet for free use on July 7, 1994. The program's name was an abbreviation of "Layer 3 Encoder." This, in turn, came from the name of the sound compression standard, established by Frauenhofer, along with experts in video and sound engineering, and researchers from around the world: MPEG-1 Layers 3. To complete this series of abbreviations, let me mention that MPEG stands for *Motion Picture Expert Group,* a team of experts who gathered in 1998 to create standards for the movie industry in order to get more digital content to the consumers, using less space – for example, on DVDs where the video standard is MPEG-2. MPEG-1 was the first video standard from this team of experts and the third layer in the description of the standard was the sound. What that little free program, *L3enc,* could do was to compress sound according to the conditions described in the MPEG-1 standards third layer. For that very reason, it was logical that the product that came out of it was entitled *.mp3.* As so often before, there weren't many people at Frauenhofer who had seen the revolution coming which the MP-3 phenomenon would soon become. Before July of 1994, few people had even considered loading the content of their CDs into their computers. Why would you? Although the CDs were digital, it wasn't just a matter of transferring them to files on the computer. The computers had no, or had bad, speakers. And the content of a CD would easily take up 600 to 700 megabytes which, at the time, would occupy much of the available "real estate" on the built-in hard discs of those beige machines. It would only be possible to have one – maybe two – CDs on the computer, after which there wouldn't be space left for anything else on the drive. But nonetheless people would experiment; and it didn't take long before computer nerds started toying with running their CDs through *L3enc. L3enc* could compress the music to a tenth of its size, so that a whole CD would take up 40 to 50 megabytes instead of 600. With a little tweaking and fixing you could make your machine play these mp3-files. And then if you added external speakers or headphones to the equation it would even sound good! The computer geeks of the world started seeing the potential of mp3. One of the things that really drove it home was, that it was possible to extract only the songs you liked from a CD, then put them in a folder with other favorite tunes, thus creating your own jukebox on the computer. The mp3 phenomenon caught on. College students would send mp3 files to each other on their internal college networks, which were sufficiently powerful to support them – private internet hadn't come quite far enough yet. In the dorms, students skilled in computers would put up servers that could host everyone's mp3 files, for the whole house to enjoy. Then, in 1997, the company Nullsoft introduced the Winamp program, an mp3 player for the PC, sporting a nice graphics user interface, and allowing the user to organize files in *playlists* for the first time. Those playlists would be the descendants of the mix-and-match tapes many of those users had made in their childhood and adolescence. It was also around this time that the music business first started realizing that something illegal was taking place. Apart from the local servers of mp3 files, people had started uploading mp3 files to ordinary, private home pages for others to download. This was piracy of a scale not experienced since the movie industry pursued the illegal video manufacturers in the 1980s, and the software industry went after the software pirates of the 1990s. This time it was about music. The music business had tried to stop the copying of LPs to cassettes before, but had found peace in the fact that the sound quality would decrease dramatically when making such a copy, and for that reason alone it was hard to consider it an exact copy. But the mp3 quality was very close to the original, and by now the CD burner had become a household item. So the copying of CDs without conversion to mp3 was also rampant on a large scale. To understate greatly, the music business was not happy. The final blow to the recording industry of the industrial society would come in June of 1999, dealt by 19-year old programmer Shawn Fanning.

All Hail The Napster!

In 1998 Fanning was a student at Northeastern University in Boston. He and his friends would spend much of their time on the internet looking for mp3 files. Through chat clients like IRC, and the newsgroup network USENET, they could gain free access to servers that harbored loads of free music. But it was hard to navigate through the files, not least because the people who had put up the servers didn't have much sense of structure when it came to music files. You would take what you could get, once you had gained access to a server and rummaged through libraries and folders. Fanning thought it should be just as easy to search for music as it was to search for information through Yahoo, AltaVista or Lycos, which were the most cutting-edge search engines at the time. As he reasoned, you should be able to just type in the song's name, and find it. So in 1998 he started writing a program which could do just that. If you installed his program on your computer, you could invite others in and allow them to access your music collection – in return for gaining access to theirs. (The ideal reciprocal network.) The program was connected to servers that could direct music seekers to computers that had the songs they were searching for. After directing the user to the right place, the program would automatically link one's computer to the music library on the distant computer, and the songs could be transferred directly from computer to computer. This little program, which would bring the international music business to its knees, was called *Napster*. "Napster" was Shawn Fanning's nickname when he was in high school, because of his tufty "nappy" hair. During the two years *Napster* was up and running in its first incarnation, the user numbers climbed steadily to reach more than 25 million users in March of 2001. This was also the month of which an American court ordered the people behind Napster to shut down the service, after a ruling in a case filed by the American music business as far back as 1999, 5 months after Napster had been set free on the internet. A year and half later the court ruled in favor of the music business, and Napster was shut down in July of 2001. But by then the damage was done, or the revolution had happened, depending on your point of view. After Napster came more so-called *peer-to-peer* or P2P clients (named after the direct connection through which the computers share information), like Limewire or Morpheus which ran on the fully distributed network Gnutella. And then there was KaZaA, which

190

in its structure resembled Napster by having a central "switchboard," created by the Dane Janus Friis and the Swede Niklas Zennström, who would later use their experience from KaZaA to give the world (nearly) free telecommunications through Skype. Today it is primarily place like the Usenet and Bittorrent networks that are predominant. Napster and the P2P revolution brought the music business – or at least the royalty-based aspect of the music business – to rack and ruin. In most of the western world, CD sales peaked in the year 2000. Only five years later in 2005, CD sales were cut in half. The trend was the same all over the world. The youth had spoken. They would no longer pay what, to them, seemed like *too much* for a CD, which had maybe only two songs on it that they liked. Music to them was almost like a human right, something which they should be able to use like water from a faucet, as the German music futurist Gerd Leonhard has put it. This was what illegal downloading services could offer – music as readily available as water. The music business tried out many alternatives, but all based on payment. In the beginning of the year 2000 I personally triggered an initiative to unite the recording industry with artists' organizations in order to create a legal alternative to Napster. Nine years and many evolutionary steps later, this is one of the largest distributors of digital music in Scandinavia, under the name Basepoint Media. But it is still a service that works in return for payment, and where files are protected against copying. Apple advanced the process in 2003 by opening iTunes Music Store, where internet surfers could buy music for the iPod. The wide selection, and the ease of purchase, turned it into a massive success – even though it wasn't free. This is an important point, which I will get back to. In January of 2009 Apple finally removed the copy protection from most of their music files. CD sales kept plummeting as more and more people downloaded illegal music from the internet. According to the recording industry organization IFPI's *Digital Music Report* from 2011, revenue from sales of music recordings has dropped by 31% globally over from 2004-2010. In Europe, at least one in four active internet users download illegal music. In Spain and

Brazil that number is almost half of the internet-connected population. As the report has it:

"Further studies reinforce this point. A 2010 study by Adermon & Liang of Uppsala University, Piracy, Music and Movies: A Natural Experiment, ...found physical sales would be 72 per cent higher in the absence of piracy, which accounted for 43 per cent of the drop in sales between 2000 and 2008. Digital music sales would be 131 per cent higher in the absence of piracy."

To put it differently: *Music consumption is greater than ever but it is still primarily illegal.* Is it because people are scroungers who don't want to pay for the music? That's not necessarily the case. In the past few years many free music alternatives have been introduced. You can listen to music free with sites like Pandora, Grooveshark and Last.FM and with sites like Spotify in Europe, you can even choose the songs you want to hear. Recently, as mentioned, telcos have started offering totally free, on-demand music downloads to their customers. As long as you are a loyal customer, you can listen to the music on your cell phone or broadband-connected computer. Yet *still,* people all over the world keep downloading music illegally. Why? Because, once again, it isn't the price of $0.00 that is important to the people out there. Apple got it right with iTunes. By making you type in your credit card *once* and then forget about it, it is easier than ever to buy a song. And since you can do it with one or two clicks, do it from your cell phone or your tablet, it's actually *easier* than engaging in illegal activity. And in contrast to the illegal services, you know the sound quality of the music is going to be acceptable, and you don't get any viruses attached to your download. But when you buy music off iTunes or listen to one of the many free, on-demand streaming services, you are consuming music in a way that rivals the illegal sites in convenience. And you are actually even paying for it. It just doesn't feel that way.

As mentioned earlier, the largest online music store, The Apple iTunes Store, started selling most of its music *without* copy protection. This is something the runner-up on the list, *eMusic.com,* had done for quite some time. It had secured them a healthy turnover, even though the selection of music was limited to the artists that were on independent labels. Apple had already won the race by making the most convenient solution of all. The iTunes program, which corresponds to the world's leading MP3 player phenomenon, the iPod, was the most user friendly program of its kind when it came out. It just worked, and it was very intuitive... which is to say, *convenient.* When Apple launched its music store, it wasn't as an external web page, but as an integral part of iTunes, which everyone with an iPod had already installed on their computers. This made it easy to buy, download, and transfer songs to the player in a jiffy. Competitors weren't able to match this product, and that level of convenience created the success of the iTunes Store. The process of purchasing music was also incredibly convenient. It was simply a matter of punching one's credit card information into a profile. When it was time to buy something, it was just a question of choosing it and confirming the purchase. This was easier than any of the competitors' solutions, which usually involved typing in credit card information again for each new purchase. The profile solution was also far more convenient than having to leave the house, go to a record store, and stand in line to wait for service by a sales person.

Once Again: It's Not About The Money. It's about the payment process obstructing one's flow.

The conclusion is that *the illusion of free is important.* After a couple of years of recession, we have learned the hard way that there is no such thing as a free lunch (not even from some ever expanding equity in your house). Even though the proponents of the free/gift economy have misunderstood how the notion of free really works in the reality of our network society, Richard Stallman, Chris Anderson and the other "freebees" are right that things must *appear* to be free. *The illusion of free* is one of the most important marketing tricks in the network society, because Homo Conexus *demands* the feeling of free. But behind this feeling is another term which is even more important to understand, when one wants to know how to perceive Homo Conexus as a consumer. We touched upon this before, but we will know dig into this phenomenon in all of its lazy splendor: *convenience.*

CHAPTER TEN:

CONVENIENCE IS KING

If you look up the word "convenience" in The Merriam-Webster Online Dictionary, four different meanings pop up, all pointing in the same direction, namely something that makes something else easier. Or as the fourth suggestion has it: freedom from discomfort. When I choose to use the word convenience, it isn't just because the leading commercial analysts of the world use it. It's also because the word has a ring of comfort, accessibility and ease. The classic trade-off of trading has always been price versus quality. How much can quality cost; what is good quality; and how much can you afford to let quality go down in order to boost sales volume? In the Industrial Society there has always been a rather predictable relation between the two parameters: The lower the quality, the lower the price. You want quality, you need to pay more. Some claim that you can easily find good quality that's inexpensive – many would say, for instance, that it is perfectly possible to find a great bottle of wine for around $6– you just need to look for it. But no matter how "lucky" one may be, subjectively, in a situation like that, there is still one basic fact: If a maker has spent hours of skilled labor, and used high quality durable materials to create a product, it has to cost a lot – otherwise he can't make a living. Many have lived by the phrase "I am willing to pay for good quality," based on the presumption that good quality means durability, therefore less need to replace the product within a short time. Shoes are a good example – expensive shoes usually last longer. And if they don't, it's probably because there was an add-on that needed to be paid for with the purchase: trendiness. In the world of fashion, things are usually much more expensive than the quality would seem to justify. But the distance between price and quality is usually bridged by trendiness. You are also paying to bolster your personal image (and probably also your self-esteem) when you pay exorbitant prices for high fashion items. Neuro-marketing experts claim that the ego boost derived from the purchase of these fashion items, releases chemical rewards in the brain that make the body feel good. Whether these chemical rewards are released because one's self-perception is improved, or the other way around, is not important. In the price/quality context this added value is a part of the quality of the product, when you pay a little extra for it. Price and quality still go together in the fashion world. But with the appearance of Network Society, a third player joins the game. In between these two fundamental sales parameters, convenience squeezes in. It's a parameter that is just as important as the two others, as we will now see. It used to be enough to convince Industrial Society customers of a given item's attractive price or high quality. However, now Homo Conexus demands convenience as well. But isn't the convenience parameter just another part of the item's quality? No, whereas quality related product properties like design, usability, trendiness or customer relevance all pertain to the product itself, the convenience parameter is defined by the product and by the network it enters into. It is as much the product's properties in relation to the reality around it that create its convenience. Further, we can also say that a product isn't convenient when it comes from the factory. It needs to enter into a context in order to become convenient. A product's level of convenience is determined by its ability to adapt to the times; its availability in the market; how its brand message is communicated; and its ease of use. Convenience can be as important to a purchase as price and quality, even though convenience as a purchase driver has entered seriously into the equation only with the coming of Network Society. Certain products are so convenient that people are willing to pay a premium price. They are so convenient that people are willing to let quality be quality, and still pay a premium price. Convenience doesn't beat price in every case, but right now it's more important than quality in many cases. For instance: There is strong evidence that a Homo Conexus native would rather patronize a store that makes his or her life easier. In May 2010, a survey conducted by WebVisible and Synovate showed that consumers in general prefer small business instead of chain stores. Only 17% of the respondents did not prefer shopping at their small, local store rather than driving to a less expensive Big Box retailer or mall outside of town. 19% said it was because they wanted to support their local community. But nearly just as many, 17%, claimed the reason was that "The local merchant is more conveniently located". Conveniently located. Even in a time where money is tight, consumers prefer convenience over saving money. This tendency was also evident to The National Association of Convenience Stores in 2008. Convenience stores usually are smaller places with a wide selection, staying open when it's convenient for customers to pick up what they need. Of course, the name Convenience Store gives away that it's all about being convenient. But at a time when American warehouse operations have the possibility of buying, or having goods produced, in the Far East, and selling them to American consumers, it is nevertheless surprising that local, one man shops could be thriving. But they were. As a matter of fact the turnover in smaller local stores went up 1.4% from 2007 to 2008, even with fierce competition from the big and very inexpensive warehouses. That smaller stores were losing money because credit card companies were already feeling the recession, and raised their fees, is another matter. The recession is likely to cool down the trend for a couple of years, during which time people will have more price awareness. But with so many factors pointing in the same direction, it seems safe to conclude that the convenience tendency will return along with the return of consumer optimism. The indicators are many. Just check out these following examples where convenience beats price and quality:

Flat Screen TVs

Remember when flat screen TVs first came out? In spite of high definition (HD) television still not being available everywhere, we all ran out and got them. Regular, standard television on flat screen monitors normally doesn't compare to the image quality of tube television. Even so, flat panel TVs went flying off the shelves, and people decided to dish out the considerable price difference between a flat screen monitor and a standard TV set. The price is higher, and the quality of the image lower, as long as what is being watched is standard television, not HD. But a flat screen is very convenient. You don't need to arrange your living room furniture based on where the TV set is placed, because it doesn't take up the usual 1-2 feet of space behind it. You can just hang it on a wall. Furthermore, you don't need to worry about what else to hang there. Often, but not always, the flat screen design is nicer than that of a tube television. Apart from that design element, there is the context in which the flat screen monitor exists, making it convenient and desirable – quite apart from any consideration of price or quality.

Bottled Water

Bottled water is another excellent example of how convenience trumps price and quality. In 1999, the environmental interest group National Resource Defense Council (NRDC) ended a four-year study of bottled water compared to tap water and concluded that

"No-one should assume that just because water comes from a bottle that it is necessarily any purer or safer than most tap water."

Another 22% of the bottles actually contained contaminated water, as defined in the regulatory levels set by the state of California. And yet, as the report also states, most Americans

"...are willing to pay 240 to over 10,000 times more per gallon for bottled water than we do for tap water."

Once again, it's neither low price nor high product quality – or even the relation between the two – that makes us buy bottled water. Bottled water is convenient. It's mobile water. It's water on demand. It's a hassle to carry around a big jug of water, having to refill it from time to time. And besides, public drinking fountains aren't exactly very appealing. This convenience factor makes people not care about the environment; pay through the roof; and even settle for lower quality. And if you're thinking "Well, wasn't it always like that?" then try to recall, when you were a kid, when you ever drank from small bottles of water from France, Scotland or Norway on an everyday basis. Right. Didn't think so.

IKEA

The furniture giant IKEA is a cult phenomenon with its own fan websites and a successful and sustainable company culture. They, also, are masters of convenience. In its native Scandinavia, IKEA is branded across the shopping culture. Many Scandinavians have been IKEA customers since their parents dragged them to their local warehouses as kids. They need to really dredge their memories to remember a furniture purchase that didn't require some kind of assembling. The most convenient furniture purchase one can make is to go to a store, point out the furniture, and have it delivered (or buy it online). Yes, to some people this is inconvenient, because occasionally an item can't be delivered on the day of the purchase – but let's continue the thought for the sake of the experiment. Having furniture delivered and carried into the house usually costs more than buying furniture from IKEA. For obvious reasons: IKEAs solution has saved manpower on the assembling of the furniture, and on mover costs. So if you have the money, you can buy convenience without ever coming near those huge blue and yellow concrete boxes just outside the cities. Price may still be the primary reason that people shop for furniture at IKEA. But price doesn't do it alone. Author Douglas Coupland has labeled IKEA's products Swedish Semi-Disposable Furniture. Low quality furniture, meant only to last short-term. So, it isn't the high quality and durability that sells the product. Then it must be the price, right? Not exclusively, if we are to believe studies from Harvard Business School, and articles in serious media such as Business Week. First off, IKEA is very good at something that started this chapter; the illusion of free. Nothing at IKEA is really free – not even the very convenient babysitting benefit of dumping the kids at the supervised playroom. But there's still a sense that everything is so inexpensive that it is almost free. And so, one fills the basket or cart until arriving at the register only to find out that a lot more money has been spent than what was originally the intention. Did you ever do that? Bertille Faroult did, a customer in IKEA in Paris, who said the following to Business Week:

"They have this way of making you believe nothing is expensive."

IKEA's business model corresponds very well with the illusion of free – a big part of the convenience concept is precisely a matter of concentrating on picking out the right items, and not worrying about the final bill. IKEA achieves this illusion by mixing incredibly cheap items with more expensive ones, in a way that doesn't highlight the expensive ones. Most stores have their more expensive items placed in designated spots. Expensive wines are often placed high on market shelves; costly designer brands often have their own designated part of the clothes store or warehouse. But IKEA invented a different shopping psychology that leads customers "around the house." All IKEA stores in the world are the same, with a very visible, almost circular, navigation. As described by Krystyna Gavora, an architect from Schaumburg, Illinois:

"Because the store is designed as a circle, I can see everything as long as I keep walking in one direction."

Surprising words from an architect, who shouldn't be daunted by structural challenges within buildings. This convenience-oriented way of perceiving the IKEA experience means that the customer focuses on the navigation of the store – not on the price of certain items compared to others. You're taken by the hand and don't have to think too much. Therefore you can focus on the items you're looking for, and not so much on whether they're in the cheap or the more expensive side of the warehouse. By making IKEA shopping extremely convenient, IKEA has diverted the customer's attention from the price as well as the quality.

Mobile Applications

Since work on this book began, the market for small programs for your "smart phone" has grown at an explosive pace. The merging of the pocket PC and the cellular phone that became the smartphone started back in 2003. Since then, software producers have developed programs and games which can be installed on phones. These applications range from bus schedules and programs to help small business owners track expenses and inventory; to music and video players. But it nearly took a master's degree in Nerdiness 101 to install those programs. Apple changed all that with the introduction of the convenient App Store for the iPhone. Apple's business model is to make things simple for everyone to use. And just as they made purchasing music more convenient than before, they simplified the process of installing little programs with App Store, giving ordinary people access to mobile applications. They were buying software just as they were buying music on iTunes – on impulse and with a great level of convenience. This created a huge market for those little programs. As of January 2011, there are more than 400,000 iPhone apps that can either be downloaded for free, or bought at very low cost. Nokia, Samsung, and other mobile phone manufacturers and software companies have joined the game, because now there is a market.

Apps are now on TVs, game consoles and other consumer electronics. There are even app stores on computers. Instead of going online to buy your software, you just repeat the same experience you just had on the phone. Codeword once again:

Convenience. Even Google and Microsoft decided to get in the game with their own smart phone operating systems. Google has made a fortune creating free, easy applications for the PC which become venues for advertising. There was no way they were going to let Apple get away with hogging the mobile sector of that marketplace. Hence, Android and the Android market was born. Then Microsoft got their act together and brought apps to the Zune marketplace and created the more user friendly operating system Windows Phone 7 for phones. Smartphones had existed for over five years – an eternity in this speed-crazed technological atmosphere – before mobile applications became convenient enough to create a mass market. It took the emergence of convenience to get customers crowding the stores. When Apple started marketing their apps, they realized this. Hence, the payoff for their U.S. TV commercials was, "Solving life's problems – one app at a time." So, Apple specifically marketed the applications on convenience.

Digital Entertainment

Whether it's a question of furniture, food supplies or consumer electronics, it all revolves around convenience these days. But in no other area is the emphasis on convenience more evident than in the case of entertainment products. As I mentioned earlier, the illegal downloading of music helped push us further into Network Society, because it put focus on how important sharing is to Homo Conexus, and because it put the illusion of free on the map. But convenience also owes its fair share to Napster and the MP3 revolution. Let's look at the concept of quality first. Sound quality was once an important factor in music, but today it has given way to convenience – like so many other quality factors. Studio techs and music producers around the world are pulling out their hair, when they hear the music they have toiled with using expensive studio gear, played back as over-compressed MP3 files through computer speakers. The young Homo Conexus will even gladly listen to music from the tiny, nasal speaker in a phone – much to the agony of nearby listeners. This latter example takes places for two reasons, however: Because it is important to share the experience, which is hard to do using headphones, and because it is more convenient. The cell phone goes everywhere you do, and if it's just a matter of sometimes listening to a little music together it is very inconvenient to lug around a boom box. But even before the latest pop hit has traveled very far, it has been cut to 10% of its size by compression into the MP3 standard. 90% of the information in the digital version of the music has been discarded, which has to affect the quality of the sound.

Homo Conexus doesn't care.

It's more important to him or her to be able to take the music with them, and share it with others, because this accumulates social currency and keeps the connections vibrant. On top of that, the general decentralization of reality means that the very idea of listening to a whole album by one single artist is a very special experience, something done only seldom. It's like the difference between watching a movie on TV or in the theatre. The movie theatre is a special experience, something one doesn't do very often. There's a trend right now of young people buying vinyl records like never before – precisely for those few, intimate times. But the mass market is still MP3, because that's what's most convenient. So, what happens when the music purchase becomes inconvenient? Well, as I have discussed earlier, the illegal alternative becomes even more tempting. Many studies have shown that even young people today are willing to pay for music, especially if it can be purchased online. But there can't be a slowdown between the desire to buy and the purchase itself. It needs to be instant gratification. Music buyers don't buy music to own it. They buy it in order to be able to listen to it, and the more irritating steps they encounter between the initial interest and the listening experience, the more convenient the illegal alternative seems. As mentioned, there's also the important concept of sharing. Until recently it was nearly impossible to buy music on the internet that wasn't copy protected by Digital Rights

Management, which made it a hassle to transfer the music to another computer; to one's MP3 player; or to share it with friends. The latter is of course illegal, but nevertheless it is a part of the music ritual of many teenagers. This was previously done with cassette tapes. For today's young Homo Conexus, especially, it's of vital importance, because music is one of the most important kinds of social currency that can be exhanged in order to keep connections vibrant in a relationship. Music is one of the most important social currencies there is. The same goes for the victims next in line when it comes to internet piracy: Film and television companies. By now films can be downloaded illegally just like music, and almost as fast. Then you can watch the movies on your laptop, or connect it to the flatscreen TV in your home "cinema" and watch on that. Still, few people would prefer to trek down to the store when they can to stay inside; sit in the kitchen wearing only their underwear; while the computer downloads that latest blockbuster in a mere 20 minutes – as they attend to the cooking. This mode of delivery is simply so convenient that it beats DVD rentals or purchases, even if it means watching the flick on a computer instead of the TV. Netflix revolutionized convenient movie watching by first bringing the movie to you through the mail, then as a streaming service online. But not just any service. You can watch Netflix on almost any game console you have hooked up to your TV, and if you are on the move, you can watch Netflix movies on your phone or tablet. What's the idea behind Netflix payment system? You pay a fixed amount every month…and then you just view as many movies as you wish. Netflix is really the embodiment of how to sell something to Homo Conexus with successfully. Forget about quality, but make the delivery and payment convenient. Netflix's streaming service is now so popular that they are hinting towards an end to their DVD-rental service in a not too distant future. This was the service that brought the mighty Blockbuster chain to its knees. Blockbuster went down because they never tried to compete on convenience. The reality: Homo Conexus will always reach for the most convenient alternative. Whatever that is at the time. Even watching TV fiction has changed. We TiVo our favorite shows and watch them when it's convenient. Sometimes we'll even let a few episodes accumulate so we can watch several episodes in one sitting. If we don't just watch them on Netflix or iTunes, of course. In other words, convenience is the key factor in the choice of many, if not all, relatively inexpensive consumer goods. Price is obviously not out of the game. But it is losing its longtime position as the most important determinant. A survey from the American price comparison service Shopzilla shows that customers who thought that price was "the most important" purchase driver, had dropped from 59% in 2003 to 49% in 2007. And again, even though the financial meltdown has boosted price awareness among consumers, evidence suggests that this is hardly likely to stop the trend. Only pause it for a couple of years.However, price still is a consideration when it comes to major investments like cars or houses. It's hardly a general principle that people choose an expensive car over an inexpensive one because it is more convenient. But convenience has become a key factor as opposed to many other relating to the car. When was the last time you rolled down the windows in a modern car using the old fashioned handle? Power windows have become a high priority in a car because they make the use of the vehicle more... well, convenient.

When Social Networks Meet E-Commerce

A new tendency emerging in the purchase patterns of Homo Conexus is *shopping in networks*. Instead of shopping for clothes in an online store, or driving over to the mall to hang out with your physical network, and be networking with new potential possessions, you can also join social networks that focus on buying. A perfect example is gilt.com. Gilt Group is an online clothes network, through which one can purchase expensive brands and exquisite designs for a fraction of the price. If you become a member, that is. Because it isn't a network anyone can use just like that – you have to be invited in by another member. In this way, the Gilt network remains a "place" for a select group of people who actually wish to buy clothes that are somewhat more luxurious than those available in your everyday town shopping plaza. It may sound odd that the merchant doesn't want to reach as large a body of customers as possible. But as a matter of fact it makes perfect sense. The super high-end Italian fashion brand Prada recently revealed that 50% of the company's clothes were bought by just 5% of their customers. Once again it is the "few-to-many" principle at play, just as in the case of Wikipedia and YouTube. To put it differently: If prestige apparel brands get most of their profit from a small group of customers willing to pay extra money, then why spend on big, broad marketing campaigns and hassle with an irritating and uncertain retail sector? Many of the right people are gathered in these networks anyway. Brands that normally have trouble putting their items on sale because of the fear of devaluating their exclusivity can reduce inventories by marketing through Gilt, which is already *available only to the few, right people.* Brand equity is thereby maintained even as overstock is being dumped – the best of both worlds! To Homo Conexus this is super convenient. They know where they can always find the right goods, without having to deal with crowds of sale-trippers when the sales begin. The networking structure of this style of shopping also appeals to Homo Conexus. In the case of Gilt there is another appealing feature: The goods are up for sale only short term, by agreement with the clothes brands. By controlling sales in this way, Gilt can order only merchandise that has already been sold. They don't have to spend money on expensive storage space. This type of e-business is what evolves when social networks and e-commerce are combined. The phenomenon is called *Social + Premium*, and it is spreading like wildfire right now. It's what happens when you pay real money for certain features and virtual goods in games on Facebook, like *Farmville*. The same idea is behind Groupon, which offers a *convenient* way for people to group together and get volume discounts on everything from travel to groceries. It's part of the business model for Foursquare – you spend your money at a place recommended by the social network. Gilt simply has the element of exclusivity included in the formula.

This exclusivity is a sign of another tendency that's catching on – the *decentralization of social networks* which, over time, will presumably become smaller and increasingly interest-based. Because, as we saw in Chapter Eight, one can only have 150 real friends. That is why Homo Conexus doesn't like to network on sites like eBay, no matter how much they try to come off as social networks. If you go to eBay's front page, you'll find they have a "Community" section now. But eBay is a place you buy stuff. Not a venue for socializing. It's not an authentic social network. And, as I will discuss, authenticity is crucially important to Homo Conexus when he or she receives commercial messages or goes shopping.

Authenticity Always Wins

If all options are available, who would choose the option where they will be cheated? It may seem simplistic to put it this way, but many marketing people are still willing to blatantly lie to Homo Conexus, just to gain access to their wallets! Whole segments of the marketing industry are still living back in Industrial Society. They continue to believe that massive media exposure is best; that bad press is better than no press; and that it still can be beneficial to lie to get their products or services sold. These presumptions are not just wrong and old-fashioned; they are self-destructive.One of the most important things that has happened to change consumer values in the new Network Society, is the increase in the availability of a huge variety of products. The supply of media – marketing channels – has become similarly vast. The number of media that Homo Conexus is in touch with every day is also much greater than it used to be, especially since many of those are social media. The supply of products from all over the world has also expanded due to globalization. Further, the technical revolution has made it possible for anything that can be sold digitally to stay on virtual "store shelves" indefinitely. The amount of available entertainment products (games, movies, music, software) just keeps growing, with hardly any content being discontinued. Some products have even become less expensive for that same reason. Never before has there been such a cornucopia of opportunities when it comes to choices individual consumers can make, limited only by their income bracket and desired level of convenience. This has naturally caused some noise in the marketing arena. More products = More marketing. And from this tendency an interesting change now emerges. People are shopping more and more with their *hearts:* With their emotions: With their right brains. Marketing guru Martin Lindstrom deals with this subject in his book *Buy-ology*, in which he shows to what extent *feelings are essential* to the purchase process. He describes his own research, and the neuroscientific research of others, into the field of consumption. The scientists he has worked with, and others he refers to, have all gauged people's brain activity in different marketing situations. Feelings – not the rational process; not even common sense – prove to be the central factor in the decision to purchase a product, and a key factor in the positive reception of an advertising message:

"...all of which serves to evoke associations of collaboration and partnership of you and the product embarking on a journey together, hand in hand. Remember, the road to emotion runs through our sensory experiences...emotion is one of the most powerful forces in driving what we buy."

Elsewhere in the book, Lindstrom describes an experiment in which a group of students was offered a gift certificate for $15 on *Amazon.com* if they accepted it *immediately*. But if they waited two weeks, they could have a certificate for $20. In nearly every case, the emotional boost of getting the certificate *here and now*, was more important to the respondents than getting an additional 20% of monetary value.

"Of course, their rational minds knew the $20 was logically a better deal but – guess what? – their emotions won out."

Homo Conexus feels the same way, of course. They feel that way to a great extent. Because Homo Conexus natives have always been used to having the world at their fingertips, they have also grown used to *instant gratification.* Martin Lindstrom's example shows how it is more important to move on along the path of one's networking journey quickly and easily, than it is to do it inexpensively. And if there's something that can really be a hindrance to that process, it is feeling suspicious. If Homo Conexus becomes the least bit suspicious in regard to a product someone is selling, the product will not have nearly as good a chance as it would have had with an Industrial Society native. Because to find out the true value of a product takes research, including consulting with your peers. And that "due diligence" is the opposite of instant gratification. Why not just take the product right next to it, which, because of its honest appearance and communication, speaks directly to one's feelings – even if it is a little more expensive? The overwhelming supply of commercials and products has made Homo Conexus an eagle-eyed consumer who spots "fake" immediately. Because the "real" product is right next to the not-so-real one. The products and brands which are gaining ground are doing so because they're either very good at appearing as authentic, or because they *really* are. Apple, for instance, has prospered tremendously during the emergence of Homo Conexus. This is partly because their products are convenient like none other, but also because they fulfill Martin Lindstrom's premise of going through the senses to reach the feelings via the superior designs. But it is also a question of authenticity: "Designed by Apple in California," has long appeared on the packaging of the company's products. Apple isn't an American company, it's a *Californian* company, with all of the connotations that come along with that statement: Sunshine, surfing, juicy oranges, beautiful nature, prosperity, Silicon Valley and Hollywood. All emotion-engaging images. Forget that Apple products are really manufactured by Foxconn in China (which in 2006 was criticized for maltreating its employees!). And never mind that the entire music industry felt that they were cheated by Apple boss Steve Jobs and his company's totalitarian pricing in the iTunes Music Store, which at one point practically held a monopoly on digital download sales. Despite all that, Apple's image remains untouchable because of its brilliance in communicating to consumers' *feelings*, and their willingness to show the world how much they loved their own products. How much more honesty can be achieved than the CEO of a company standing up and, not only telling but also showing how much he loves his brand's products? Douglas Rushkoff also comments on the matter:

"We've become so sophisticated now, that if a company says they stand for a certain quality, there are plenty of people who will investigate it and let people know if the company is telling the truth. Even if an individual doesn't have the resources to do this work, then that person now knows where to find out if a company, say, claims to be more green than it really is."

Rushkoff also says that social currency, so important in marketing a brand today, is very much shaped by the activities of the company. He told me how Mountain Dew tried during the 2008 presidential election campaign, to jump on the "social responsibility" bandwagon, and pre-empt for the brand the tide of democratic awareness that Barack Obama had sparked in young American voters.

They failed. Why?

According to Rushkoff,

"Social Currency is created through the real actions of a company. And you just can't fake it anymore. For example, the 2008 "Dewmocracy" campaign from Mountain Dew was a huge failure. They created this web page where people could have their say about which the color and taste of the next Mountain Dew product. They did it in connection with the presidential election and tried to make it look like a way for young people to be part of a democratic process. The company got so much bad

press that it had to fire their PR firm and hire a new one to tell everyone that it was meant as a joke. You just can't do that sort of thing anymore. You can be cynical and honest, but you can't be honest without being honest."

If you want to sell something to Homo Conexus, it had better be done honestly, or at least you had better be so good at *faking honesty* that no one can tell the difference! The more offers they can examine, the better the chances that Homo Conexus can blow the cover of a phony. Authenticity and convenience that leads to instant gratification are the two most important characteristics of a successful communication with Homo Conexus. Especially if you are trying to market a product. Nobody understands this better than legendary toy manufacturer LEGO.

LEGO – Authenticity And Networks

One of the best ways of meeting Homo Conexus in the market place is to enter into Homo Conexus's own networks, if possible. There aren't many children in the Western world who are not familiar with LEGO. But even an established brand like LEGO lost its market position somewhat around the turn of the millennium. The old bricks were up against the internet; TV; gaming consoles; computers; trading cards – not to mention an array of toy merchandising concepts, some backed by complete worlds of cartoons, TV series, print campaigns and even storytelling, in an all-out pitched battle (supported by huge media expenditure) for the attention of the Homo Conexus children. For the first time in many years things were looking bleak for the renowned Danish family-run company. So they made a decision to do something they had never done before. A marketing expert was hired to be head of the company who was *not* a part of the Kirk-Christiansen family, which had founded LEGO. This person was Jorgen Vig Knudstorp, who became CEO in 2004, and then did something very modern: *He didn't try to be modern.* Instead he got LEGO back on the trail of old-fashioned honesty and credibility:

"We had ventured too far from what we were really all about - in an effort to appeal to more customers. And on the way we lost ourselves. At the same time, others went in and represented what we had stood for, and they did it as well as we had. The cure was to get back on the track of doing what we stand for, and then really focus intensely on that. We have gotten really clear about the fact that we're not for everyone. We're for those who want to build with LEGO, and we focus on delivering to those who are crazy about LEGO, and not those who don't really care so much for creative play."

The strategy worked. In 2008, after a four-year implementation of the strategy, LEGO broke its own growth record in spite of a world-wide financial crisis. Knudstorp looks typically Scandinavian – tall, blond and with glasses that say scholar rather than businessman. But make no mistake. Knudstorp may be a scholar, who holds a Ph.D., but he earned his degree in Economics, and he was only 35 years old when he became head of LEGO. So it isn't so strange that Knudstorp, being relatively young for a CEO, is also very interested in networks. Networks pop up all over the place when one takes a closer look at LEGO. When it comes to how the company's employee benefits plan is structured, how the business model looks, or how it interacts with children in real life. But it all started with a network of adults:

"We found out that there was a diehard network of LEGO users who had organized themselves in things like LUGNet, the LEGO User Group Network. Self-organized, self-financed, self-controlled. We started participating in their dialogues. Internally at LEGO this was considered as something of a shady field, somewhat strange people, weird – really. In 2003, however, we decided to embrace it. This was something we happened to come across, it had just evolved on its own. We asked ourselves how we could play a part in a meaningful way, respecting the

integrity of the LUGNet-users, but also minding the business angle for us. And I think we happened to be at the front end of what has become mainstream now, the forming of networks and communities — user generated innovation."

However, LEGO – at least as well as other companies – knows that *children have their own networks.* And in a child's network there are people, there are stories and there are toys. For some time, LEGO had tried to build its own universes, and tell its own stories. But they knew that children also get massive story input from other sources. Like George Lucas, the man who created the *Star Wars* films, and who also created *Indiana Jones* with Steven Spielberg. The *Star Wars* universe, in particular, has been part of children's networks in many different ways some 30 years. So instead of trying to compete with this place in the network, LEGO did the smart thing. They realized that kids were already building *Star Wars*-inspired spaceships out of LEGO blocks, thereby connecting toys with story themselves. LEGO decided to further enable the network communication between the *Star Wars* realm and the children. This they did by creating a number of LEGO versions of *Star Wars* characters and spacecraft. There was even a computer game based on the LEGO version of *Star Wars*. This is an example of the difference between Industrial Society and Network Society. There have been computer games based on *Star Wars* since the early eighties. There have been oceans of licensing agreements in connection with the movies, from plastic action figures and spaceship replicas to novels written around the *Star Wars* arena, to *Star Wars* candy and trading cards. But it's all silo thinking: *Star Wars* as trading cards? Trading cards with *Star Wars* characters on them? Ho hum. End of story. What is interesting about the LEGO *Star Wars* game is that it isn't just a computer game based on *Star Wars*. It isn't just a brick version of *Star Wars* either. It is a computer game which is *part of* the *Star Wars* realm, where digital brick versions of spacecraft and LEGO versions of well-known characters are *the key elements.* The bricks, the computer games, and the *Star Wars* story *all merge in one product*. That's network thinking – the elements interact and communicate, instead of sitting around in separate silos. This new approach appealed to Homo Conexus kids and youth. The LEGO *Star Wars* games are still among the best-selling worldwide, and on practically all the platforms on which they are offered. But these are not the only network activities LEGO offers kids. Being agile and astute networkers, marketers at LEGO are keenly aware that there's no way to isolate children within LEGO's own network. The children's network is much more vast. So it's a question of LEGO becoming part of that network, with the honesty still up front:

"We've facilitated many networks for children. We've got My Lego Network, and Lego Factory, where you can build and share your models with others. We've got LEGO Club which has 2,5 million members. There's Bionicle.com, which is immensely popular, and we have Lego.com which has some 14-15 million daily, unique users. So, there's no question that there's a lot of communities and networking going on. But I'm not convinced that our present success is due to a network of children. I think it's more something that has to do with the characteristics which influence children today. And we believe half consists of TV and advertisements, but the other half comes from their own networks, it's information they obtain themselves."

The CEO of LEGO also explains that the company is fully aware of the inner workings of the network, like social currency and other necessities essential to keeping consumer connections vibrant:

"We're extremely aware of social currency – we call it playground currency. The most important influence on children's choice of toy is the "playground," it can be a room or it can be a school playground. Having something to swap, exchange, and to collect, share with friends, and talk about with friends is naturally very important. This is where playground currency comes in. It's got to be fun and cool, it has to have depth and possibility for

214

*further exploration. It must be easy to get started, but also hard
to reach the end of the possibilities."*

But the LEGO Company itself is also a part of a network. It is the
international network which makes it a global company, although
it has relatively few employees:

*"In an international context we're a tiny company. We have 6,000
employees but we are active in all the world's markets. By
ourselves, we're insignificant, really. We can't benefit from our
volume like the big companies do; we're not even able to access
other markets without forming partnerships. So, we must knit a
gigantic network of partners that cover the whole value chain: in
innovation, in production, in sales, in retail and so on. We need
to be able to network without limitation."*

So, good-old LEGO isn't just a company with heart, cranking out
sensible edutainment toys for children. It is also a prime example
of how an entire company's embracing of "network thinking,"
externally and internally, can lead to a very nice turnaround. This
is because it is self-evident that Homo Conexus prefers to
consume goods that fit into a network – right? It is the most
convenient thing. It's more convenient for kids to adapt LEGO's
products to their own network, than to have to build a new one
based on some new LEGO realm. It is more convenient for us to
judge things with our feelings than with our rationality, which
Martin Lindstrom has shown us. And that is also why Apple's
feminine, beautiful designs appeal to us. Just as Apple has had
great success making things more convenient, things that used
to require the talents of a computer whiz. These things are
thereby more accessible to more people. (And therefore *bought*
by more people!) It's for the sake of convenience that we set
both price and quality aside, when we shop for a flat screen
monitor. Or wait to watch a TV series until we can buy it online,
or on DVD, so that we can watch more episodes at a time, *when
we want.* With *Instant Gratification.* More than price, more than
quality, *convenience* is the most important parameter, when

wanting to sell something to, or communicate with, the consumer of the future: Homo Conexus. It is always the more convenient option that Homo Conexus will choose, when he or she navigates through the blizzard of information and attention grabbing offers which Network Society consists of. We should never forget that.

***

EPILOGUE

We live in very interesting times. The fundamental changes going on right now are changes we'll look back on through the lenses of historians with regard for their importance. As our society slowly changes from being defined by industry to be defined by networks, and as Homo Conexus emerges as a personality type, we start to see the network structure everywhere we look. Yes, it's true that we are seeing networks everywhere because we are looking for networks everywhere. But isn't that how our perception of ourselves has always evolved? Until we know how to identify something, it is kind of hard to see it. We once all thought the world was flat, since that was what we could see. But then we learned how to understand the world as being round. And suddenly that's how we believe things are, at least until some learned person discovers otherwise. 100 years from now, we might discover something about the connectedness of the world that pulls apart the network theories. It might even happen 20 years from now. But for the moment, Western science is increasingly able to make the case for what eastern wisdom has claimed for thousands of years: Everything is connected. Everything interacts. Becoming aware of this, and basing our life perspectives on it, is new to us in the West. This new combination of the strong individual in the grand network has not been possible before. And we haven't been able to see all the connections out there. This has only happened because of the acceleration of communication brought on by the internet, cell phones and other digital communication forms that are based on the network structures Paul Baran laid out in the early sixties.

These faster, digital communication forms are the glasses we needed to be able to see the world as a network. And how smaller networks make up the big ones. As mentioned in the beginning of the book, there are many out there who are fearful of the change that is going on. Nicholas Carr, in his book *The Shallows: What the Internet Is Doing To Our Brains,* claims that our brains are suffering from a syndrome of superficiality. We have lost our ability to engage deeply into something. We browse through everything. Carr makes a compelling argument, even pointing to neurological studies that support his viewpoint. However, he doesn't seem to take into account the fact that we have so much information being thrown at us that we simply *have* to react in that way. From my experience, it's not simply a question of not diving in and getting into the depth of a subject matter or a literary discussion. It's a question of reserving one's attention for the right one. It's the *threshold* that needs to be convenient, not the material itself. Once Homo Conexus is in, he's REALLY in. It just takes convenience and authenticity and a lot more effort to get him hooked. Take for example, the Harry Potter books. They were the first pop literature phenomenon that the youngest Homo Conexus'es experienced. The first one is really easy to get into. The last one is a brick of Dostoyevsky-size proportions. And anyone who knows a young World of Warcraft gamer has seen a lot of engagement. I think a lot of Carr's arguments are based on the fact that the people who get stressed over all these changes and who can't engage properly are Industrial Society people trying too hard to be Homo Conexus'es. If you are born into this society, you don't have the same kind of problems. You could even go so far as to challenge the worth of engagement as a value – is the ability to read and understand heavy literature necessarily a good thing in the Network Society? Is being able to navigate all the new sources of information maybe of higher value? Are we also seeing a decentralization here?

Carr was one of the many people polled in a study by the Pew Internet and American Life Project. In that study, which comprised 895 so-called "technology stakeholders and critics", 76 percent said that technologies such as Google would make us *more* intelligent, not less. Only 21 percent, including Nicholas Carr, disagreed. When the report came out, MSNBC.com quoted Alex Halavais, vice president of the Association of Internet Researchers:

"I think that a marginally greater number of people will be engaged in creating media — visual as well as text — and as a result, the overall literacy will increase,"...

Halavais, in an e-mail interview, said "I'm at the Digital Media and Learning conference this week, where no one would suggest the Internet and search engines are making kids less smart. It does create new issues of literacy, in the same way that the printing press created new capacities and standards of literacy."

Which brings us back to what I started out with in this book. That what is happening now is analog to Gutenberg's acceleration of information, when he invented movable type. Regardless, the fact of the matter is: there is no going back to the Industrial Age. Information is not going to become more scarce. The barrage of inputs is probably only going to increase, as is our knowledge of the physical networks in nature we have discovered over the last decade. We will have to deal with it one way or another. But in general, I believe there are more reasons to be optimistic. After all, what is perceived as annoying behavior like texting at the dinner table, is really socializing and connecting with others. Which is good. As a society, we are not growing further apart, but closer together. As a world, we are becoming smaller, because distances no longer matter as much as they did. Because old relationships can be rekindled, thanks to new technology.

Homo Conexus takes all this for granted, living a life where taking care of one's relationship with other people is equally important as taking care of oneself.

Maybe it's time the rest of us did the same.

POSTSCRIPT 2012

As always, when man takes an evolutionary or intellectual leap, the ones who are dragging their feet begin to protest. And so, after this book was published in Danish in 2009, and was translated into English in 2011, a flurry of naysayers and worriers started publishing books in order to capitalize on the fears of the people who are afraid of change. Don't get me wrong, there are many reasons to be wary of the changes going on right now. As research in to Homo Conexus progresses, we start to see the negative sides of the development, such as a severe lack of the ability to concentrate, which must now be taught at elementary school levels, and some researchers even fear that the surge in the number of kids diagnosed with Autism or ADD has its roots in the multitude of media outlets on offer and the massive onslaught of information available. It remains to be seen whether this is the case, but it is certainly worth examining. Some authors have gotten a lot of attention on and sold a lot of books based on less well-documented argumentes. I will deal with a few of them below.

Fear and loathing in the digital age

On July 7th, 1890, The New York Times published an article entitled *In The Locomotive's Path – Early Prejudice Against Steam Railroads*. The article is a nostalgic, almost humorous look back upon events that had occurred some 60 years before, when the railroad system was slowly spreading across America. The unnamed writer cites some great examples of the absurd criticism and trepidation that railroads were met with at the time. This is perhaps the most amusing one:

"…and while one writer ("Wood on Railroads," 1825) declared that it was nonsense to expect to travel by steam at the rate of twelve miles an hour, another of the same period could see nothing to hinder one hundred miles an hour, and to show the

danger of such motion asks: "Reader, how would like to be put into a box like a coach or sedan chair and dropped from a window in the fifth or sixth flat of a house? A speed of twenty-two miles an hour is equal to thirty-two feet per second, or the velocity acquired by a descent of sixteen feet. With proper caution this, or something a little greater, may be attempted, but till we have bones of brass or iron or better methods of protecting them than we have now, it is preposterous to talk of fifty or sixty miles an hour as a practical thing."

Think of that the next time you hit 65 on the freeway.

Nowadays, we often amuse ourselves by laughing at what people in the past thought the future would look like. We shake our heads and smile when we hear about how a former head of IBM has said that the world only needs five computers (a quote that's apparently a myth) or that in the year 2000, we would all have personalized jetpacks. What fascinates me about the New York Times article is that it also pokes fun at earlier predictions and prejudices that was proved horribly, or amusingly, wrong. However, this was 1890 poking fun at 1829. How will 2070 look at 2012? Maybe I'm getting a lot of the predictions in this book wrong. Actually, there's a substantial probability that I am. In 1999, when Napster came out, I started working on the first online digital music delivery service in Scandinavia that had all the record companies on board. Back then, I told a Danish newspaper that "in five years, CDs will be gone." Boy, was I wrong. Here in 2012, people still buy CDs. In dwindling numbers, yes, but killing them off is taking a lot longer than I expected.

Bill Gates has said it the best:

"We always overestimate the change that will occur in the next two years and underestimate the change that will occur in the next ten."

The fact is, with all our technology and knowledge, we can't really predict anything. We can set up likely scenarios, but that's not the same as exact predictions. And then we can look at what goes on around us and conclude that some changes are substantial enough to have an impact on the future – whatever that impact may be. That's exactly what I'm trying to do in this book. The internet has been with us for almost 42 years now. It's probably not going away anytime soon. The same can be said about cell phones and broadcast technology, all of which constitutes a communication network that will probably live on, unless Earth gets hit by a meteor. We can also point to changes that have happened, especially in the behavioral patterns of people and try to figure out which ones will stick and which won't. The idea of communicating virally in order to achieve new inspiration or to make a bold statement is likely to either evolve into something even more effective rather than just disappear. Or, like all new ideas and technologies that make a huge impact, it'll settle down, the hype will wear off and we'll use it when we need it. Take, for instance, the emergence of TV. For its time, the speed with which television entered our homes was quite rapid. Over five years, from 1946 to 1951, the number of TVs in America rose from 6,000 to 12 million. In 1955, half of all homes in America had a TV set. The year after, William Y. Elliott wrote in his 1956 book *Television's Impact on American Culture:*

"The initial impact of television on radio was well-nigh fatal... In its impact on basic decisions of the nation, television may already rival the press, the motionpicture industry, and certainly the radio industry .... By now, close to 40-million children have been born with no concept of a world without the cyclops. And it has made its mark on the changing social pattern against almost overwhelming competition for man's time...Last year, in homes with television sets...more total time was spent watching television than in any other single activity except sleep. That includes the business of making a living: A. C. Nielsen Co., marketing research organization, comes up with the startling

figure of 2.6-billion person-hours spent every week watching the screen, 1.9-billion hours in all economic pursuits."

In 1977, Claude Hall, who was then Radio-TV editor at Billboard wrote this:

"Everybody knows that radio is a dying medium. Nearly anyone who has a smattering of talent is deserting radio for [TV]. Throughout the nation radio lay apparently dying in the wake of new media's irresistible onslaught. To many, the end of radio seems near."

And two years later, legendary producer Trevor Horn as part of the pop duo Buggles, sang:

"In my mind and in my car, we can't rewind we've gone to far. Pictures came and broke your heart, put the blame on VTR...

Video killed the radio star"

In 1984, Queen echoed that sentiment in their song *Radio Gaga*:

*"So stick around cause we might miss you
When we grow tired of all this visual
You had your time, you had the power
You've yet to have your finest hour
Radio"*

Queen's statement turned out to have some substance.

Even though several other media platforms such as the net, gaming, TV and print are vying for our attention all the time, radio is still here. It's even recently come out in a new incarnation through web and cell phone radio apps and customizable radio services such as Pandora, Spotify and Soundtrckr. And in regards to Buggles commenting on how video would kill the radio star? Well it seems that radio has somewhat outlived music video television. MTV is hardly playing any music videos anymore. Music videos are now something you watch on YouTube. And a few years back, it was in fact services such as YouTube and social media which had media analysts come to a conclusion that sounded a lot like the ones drawn in the fifties, seventies and eighties as mentioned above. This time, however, everyone thought that the Internet was going to kill TV.In August 2008, inspired by the massive online coverage of the Summer Olympics in Beijing, *The Christian Science Monitor* asked:

"Is this the summer that the Internet finally kills television as we once knew it?"

In 2007, Forrester Research published a study showing that European internet users spend 14.3 hours per week online, but only 11.3 hours watching TV. Europe's broadband penetration is a little ahead in comparison to the US, which would explain that the same trend is only reaching the US now. In December of 2010, Forrester reported that for the first time ever, Americans are spending an equal amount of time on watching TV as they spend online. And, of course, for the younger generations, the scales have tipped towards internet usage already. But what seems to be missing from the equation, is the new habit of watching TV *while* you are online. Like watching TV while interacting with your laptop or your iPad, checking IMDB to see what the name of that actor was, or looking to see when you can catch that documentary you just missed. Or updating your Facebook status to reflect what you just saw, or tweeting a comment about it. In fact, only a few months before Forrester revealed that Americans spend as much time on the internet as on TV, they published a report stating that 60% of Americans use the internet and watch TV simultaneously at least once a month, and that the number is growing fast. The fact that we use the two at the same time would why other reports seem to contradict Forrester's findings about TV and internet usage being equal. According to Nielsen numbers revealed in January 2011, Americans watched more TV than ever in 2010. *Than ever.* Two things have happened. First of all, as mentioned above, we've begun using the internet *while* watching TV. But we've also just expanded the time and the amount of attention we want to use on media. We're multitasking in order to keep up with the media onslaught. Being able to multitask is a characteristic of Homo Conexus. For the rest of us, it's a little more difficult to adapt. And that's actually the reason why I've just spent a significant amount of book space going through how our fears and predictions about new technology are often wrong. The thing is, any new technology - that is not just a fad which goes away again - booms for a while and then it settles down. Like blogs. Blogs were all the rage in 2006, and everyone talked about how everyone should have one. But then the blogosphere simmered down to being a smaller group of people with something to say, and now it's found its proper level in society. The story of the railroad above is another example. It was all the rage at the turn of the 19th into the 20th century, but then cars came along, and the railroads found their place. Cars are another example. If cars were to have continued their successful growth rates of the 50s and 60s, we would all own three or four cars each now, and they wouldn't be very fuel-efficient. But because of the natural obstacle that was the oil crisis of the 1970s, car ownership found its natural level. Technology and trends balloon until they hit the ceiling or another obstacle, of which there are plenty in a complex society as ours. And then they either die and go away, or they find a suitable level to exist on. I don't use Facebook as much as I used to. I still use it a lot, because of the massive platform for communication it has become, but the novelty has definitely worn off. Now it's just something I routinely engage in, like e-mail. Or texting. Or taking pictures with my cell phone. All things that I still do, but nowhere near as much as when they first came out. This hype cycle is the natural way we adopt new concepts or new technologies. In their book *Mastering the Hype Cycle – How to Choose the Right Innovation at the Right Time*, authors Fenn and Raskino illustrates the Hype Cycle like this:

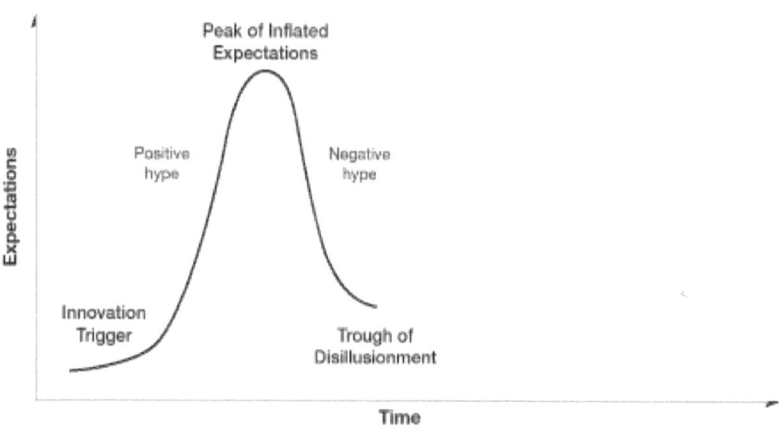

As time progresses, we get more disillusioned about the new idea, concept or product, and it is as the negative hype wears off that the survivability of this new "next big thing" is put to the test. Some, like the once overhyped virtual world Second Life, just go away. Others, like texting, survive. At the ripe age of 42, the internet is probably not going to go away anytime soon. Yet we are seeing somewhat of a backlash towards both social media and the internet these days. The internet's hype cycle really took off in the mid-nineties when the World Wide Web made it understandable and accessible to anyone. It's been a long hype cycle, and you could argue that the net first entered it's trough of disillusionment in 2000, when the web economy bubble burst. Right now, there are several thinkers and authors who are questioning the many ways we are presently communicating with each other. They feel that engaging in social media, synchronous communication like texting and IM and always having information at your fingertips isn't always for the better.

And they're right. It's not.

For better or worse

A network is value-neutral. It's a structure. You put good into it, and good things spread and happen. You put bad things into it, and you can spread evil and destruction. These faster, digital communication forms are the glasses we needed to be able to see the world as a network. And how smaller networks make up the big ones. In the west, we began a *War on Terror*, when 9/11 happened. That's really a misnomer. What we started was a war that, unlike any other war in history, wasn't against another country or large group of people. It was against *a network*. Al-Qaeda, the real target behind the War on Terror, is not an organization. It is not an ethnic group. It's not a territory. It's a network. It's a group of people, characterized by their connection to each other. We didn't start a war on a group of singular individuals with a certain idea set. No, it was *the connections between them* that threatened us, and which we felt we had to fight against. Al-Qaeda literally translates as "the list". A list of people, whose connection to each other is the fact that they are on the list together and are connected ideologically. Nowadays, we don't speak as much of Al-Qaeda as we did ten years ago. That's because Al-Qaeda has become too *decentralized* just like what happened to the second attempt at winning the Christmas no. 1 in the UK. There are those who claim that the Al-Qaeda cells who planned 9/11 never had much to do with Osama Bin Laden himself, even though he has been proclaimed the leader of Al-Qaeda. That's because Al-Qaeda was never a hierarchical structure. Rather, it is organized in the modern, decentralized group structure of the network society. And our whole Western system of war had to be reconfigured in order to change that, because we were used to fighting hierarchies.

When Hitler committed suicide in a bunker in 1945, the Nazis fell apart fast. But Osama Bin Laden is not needed for Al-Qaeda to continue living. As mentioned, Al-Qaeda has become even more decentralized recently. Many smaller terrorist networks have sprung up, making the War on Terror Networks even more difficult. The challenge of rethinking war strategies to fight within a network structure is still very present. But Al-Qaeda's organization also shows us something else. That networks really are value-neutral. They can be used for deplorable activities as well as doing good. Decentralized networks are simply strong structures between us. What we do with them is another matter. However, we must accept the omnipresence of networks. As documented in this book, scientists in medicine, biology and physics are all thinking in networks these days. One thing is fighting Al-Qaeda. But take for example the events that occurred on September 29, 2008. The American economy was imploding and the worst recession in more than six decades was starting. September 29 was the day The House of Representatives was assembled to vote on the bank bailout suggested by then president George W. Bush. No matter your ideological persuasion, that bailout was necessary, if the U.S. economy was to avoid sinking like a modern-day Titanic. Which is why one of the most right-leaning presidents in modern U.S. history decided to do something that could be characterized as downright socialist. It didn't go down well with everyone. 12 republicans decided to vote against the bailout, effectively killing this first attempt of saving the banks and thereby the U.S. economy. That's when the Network Effect kicked in. These 12 attention-grabbing republicans went on TV, online and on the radio to proclaim their objection to the bailout. With pride they told the American people how they would stick to their principles of not mixing government with the private sector if it's avoidable – even in face of an economic collapse. This happened during the day, when stocks were still being traded and the news had an immediate effect. The traders on Wall St. watched CNN proclaim that the bailout was dead, and started selling their stocks in what can only be described as a panic. This caused CNNs Wolf Blitzer to put on his most serious face as he told the world how the Dow Jones was plummeting. *That* created even a larger panic, because everyone wanted to sell before the stock values hit rock bottom. *This* was then reported by CNN, and then everything just spiraled out of control. When the stock market closed on September 29, 2008, the Dow Jones had taken its largest fall in its entire history. This is a really good example of how networks are omnipresent and almost indestructible. The political network on Capitol Hill had made a decision that was then injected into the media networks, which then again injected that information into the stock trader networks. And within the grand network that these three networks formed, information flowed so fast that no one could stop to think about what was happening and hit the brakes. The speed of communication has not just enabled us to become more connected people and think about the world in a new way. It has also opened up the possibility of disasters like we've never seen before. In the days of the ticker and the newspaper, the stock market wouldn't have been able to react fast enough to create a death spiral like the one we saw on that day in September 2008. The magnitude of the damage is increased by the speed of our networked communication. And it really shows the difference between old and new network systems. The old stock market system can't keep up with the speed of the Network Society. Add to that the positive feedback of this system, which means that the closer we get to the black hole of disaster, the faster we travel. The Network Society can accelerate the spread of both good *and* bad. This dynamic is explored, even further, by William H. Davidow in his book *Overconnected*, which provides several examples of how complex networks can be used to spread malicious information faster than ever before, and how this can have a great impact on society as such. What most of Davidows' examples have in common, though, is the fact that he is treating Industrial Age systems as if they are somehow compatible with the Network Society.

They're not, necessarily.

In fact the above example, the downward spiral of September 2008, shows how trying to maintain – and manipulate- an old system within the confines of a world that moves much faster, can go very wrong. Had the brokers and investors on Wall Street that day not just known, but really *understood* how the network and accelerated information dispersal happens, they would not have pulled the triggers as fast they did. Had CNN understood the impact they had, they would probably have handled it differently under their own rules of responsibility in journalism. The challenge here is that until you fully acknowledge what the Network Society is and understand its inner workings, you won't be able to act accordingly. And there is still a huge disparity between Homo Conexus and Industrial Man, who keeps trying to hold on to the old world. To be fair to Davidow, he does say that there are new rules in place. He just hasn't yet arrived at what they are. Trying to make Industrial Age-mechanisms work in the Network Society is bound to fail, like the proverbial square peg not fitting with the round hole. And yet there are thinkers who still seem concerned about what is going on. Like Sherry Turkle, who in her very well-researched book, *Alone Together*, leans on her many years as a researcher at MIT. She concludes that the path that we are on as we interact with machines more and more, is tearing our human-to-human interaction apart. In suggesting this, she is echoing the fears and thoughts of most people who find it difficult to understand the vast changes that are taking place. Nobody can be unsympathetic to that. These changes are so widespread and significant that it can be hard to see the whole picture. This book is all about putting those fears somewhat to rest by explaining what is going on in the broader picture. But first, let me just address some very valid concerns that Sherry Turkle brings up.

Dreading the disconnect

Turkle was one of my heroines while I was at university. She was one of the authors whose books I would use as inspiration for the research I did on how the transition into a more connected society would impact us all – even back then. I was quite disappointed of her less-than-enthusiastic stance in *Alone*

Together, and to be quite honest, my first thought was: *She should get out more*. In the first half of her book, she explores the human interactions with robotics over the years, and how she finds it uncanny that we are so willing to build relations with inanimate machines. In the book, she uses studies of kids with Tamagotchis and the virtual world of Second Life users as examples. She questions the value of people interacting virtually in Second Life as opposed to real life:

"What real-life responsibilities do we have for those we meet in games? Am I my avatar's keeper?

Am I watching a performance? Or, more probably, how much performance am I watching? Am I becoming coarsened, or am I being realistic?"

Turkle seems to be missing a very important point. *Nobody cares about Second Life anymore. Or Tamagotchis.* When Second Life was launched in 2003, it was a big deal for those who still had a remnant of the old "Virtual Reality" dream in them. After all, Virtual Reality guru Jaron Lanier (who now works for Microsoft) said in 1991 that in the long run VR was going to replace television. No sign of that happening more than 20 years later. And of course, even for all its hype, Second Life was a massive failure, and it 2010 it laid off 30% of its workforce. Among my colleagues, the media analysts, consultants and strategists I know, Second Life has been a joke for a couple of years now. We see it as some old cyberpunk dream that some very unknowing venture capitalists got some very bad advice on and decided to put money into. Having a virtual world game like World of Warcraft is one thing. There's an objective to playing that game and it works as escapism, just like movies, books or TV. But when the objective becomes to succeed in a virtual life, when most people have enough of a challenge succeeding in their real lives, it's no longer escapism, and thus less attractive. Which is why Second Life never became a success. The number of repeat users of Second Life in April 2010 was 826,214. Just to put that number in perspective, *World of Warcraft* has about thirteen times as many users as Second Life. And Facebook users now amount to well over 500 million people all over the earth. Speaking of Facebook, Sherry Turkle interviews a slew of young Facebook users in the book. At one point, she concludes that:

"Facebook at fourteen can be a tearful place. For many, it remains tearful well through college and graduate school. Much that might seem straightforward is fraught. For example, when asked by Facebook to confirm someone as a friend or ignore the request, Helen, a Roosevelt senior says, "I always feel a bit of panic… Who should I friend?… I really want to only have my cool friends listed, but I'm nice to a lot of other kids at school. So I include the more unpopular ones, but then I'm unhappy." It is not how she wants to be seen."

My question is this: Since when has it *not* been crucial to teens and young adults to be seen in a certain way, and to be acknowledged by the company they keep- Facebook or not? The problem in general with Sherry Turkle's pessimistic view that it seems to lack a good injection of common sense. First of all, she speaks almost with people who are building their identities and are finding their values in life. And to me, it seems she's confusing some of these identity issues with issues we all had growing up. Social media is just another way to reach out. When these kids grow up, they will very much have to get used to some face-to-face interaction…when they have kids themselves. You can't text your toddler to tell him to stop playing with the knives in the kitchen. Right? And at some point, it becomes more important to actually change a diaper than writing about it on Facebook. But where Homo Conexus is actually different from those who grew up in the Industrial Age, is when he or she consults the network first instead of calling Mom or Dad when baby gets sick. And decisions made on behalf of baby have the potential of being more informed than any decision our parents made. Turkle also seems to completely ignore the fact that social media and the network as such are actually being used to expand on physical experiences. She doesn't mention Flash Mobs at all, for instance. Flash Mobs is a fun trend amongst social media users to meet up and do something unexpected simultaneously at e.g. a busy train station or a town square. Look up Flash Mobs online and you will find YouTube videos of people suddenly bursting into song in great coordination, although there is no coordinator – much to the surprise of onlookers. During these fun little sessions, where people who have never met each other all of a sudden do something together, texts may fly through the air, but mostly, social media only enters the picture as people are coordinating the event beforehand on Facebook or Twitter. Another problem with Turkle's arguments is that she mostly focuses on Americans. But the Network Society is global, and as such, an American Homo Conexus feels just as much of a kinship with the German he's playing World of Warcraft with as the guy next door. Instead of consulting areas where broadband penetration and especially mobile data usage is way ahead of the US, like Scandinavia or South Korea. Turkle only ventures outside when she looks into Japan. She claims that:

"The Japanese take it as a given that cell phones, texting, instant messaging, email and online gaming have created social isolation. They see people turn away from their families to focus on their screens. People do not meet face-to-face, they do not join organizations."

But the social isolation problem in Japan did *not* start with new media. Japan has a very big problem with socially isolated youth. Dubbed the *Hikikomori,* there are now a vast number of people in Japan, who for personal or social reason become recluses, isolating themselves in their rooms or apartments. It's one of the main contributors to Japans high suicide rate. It's a very sad fact that there is a suicide in Japan almost every 15 minutes. But there's no direct correlation to the internet and other new media. At least not according to Michael Zielenziger, who wrote the book *Shutting Out the Sun* about this problem. In the book, he states that only about 10% of the *Hikikomori* spend time online when they are in isolation. It is not far-reached to conclude that for those people, getting into social media might very well be a way *out* of isolation rather than further into it. She also doesn't take into account what social media has done to the very "physical" interaction that is taking place in the Middle East right now. As I am writing this, the Egyptian government has just resigned because of demonstrations and riots inspired by what happened a couple of weeks earlier in Tunisia. Algeria may be next, in fact all over the Middle East, youth is rising up as I'm finishing this book. How do they organize demonstrations and bypass the government controlled media? You got it – Facebook, Twitter, and in particular, text messaging. It also happened in Iran not too long ago, though the government there managed to suppress the demonstrations. But something is brewing, and it's both because of and assisted by social media. It's because social media is hard to put under government control that kids in middle eastern dictatorships are able to catch a glance at what the world outside looks like. They see the freedom and wealth of their European, Russian or even American friends on Facebook. And they wonder why they can't have it too. And then they use the same media to assemble and demonstrate. That's definitely a case were social media is bringing people closer together rather than tearing them apart. Yes, there are changes in the way that we interact face-to-face, since we also started interacting digitally. But there are just as many "physical" social benefits to social media as there are drawbacks. Interacting in the physical world is not going away at all, it's just changing, and is even often enhanced by our digital interactions. Later, I'll go into greater length about how social media and other new media now help improve our physical interaction with each other. For now, let me just assure anyone who shares Sherry Turkle's and William Davidow's worries that the world is not going to hell. But it *is* changing in a big way, and to navigate the Network Society means you have to understand it, as well as its native inhabitants, Homo Conexus.